Successful Real Estate Investing in a Boom or Bust Market

Other Books by the Author

Profit by Investing in Real Estate Tax Liens: Earn Safe, Secured, and Fixed Returns Every Time

Investing in Duplexes, Triplexes & Quads: The Fastest and Safest Way to Real Estate Wealth

Successful Real Estate Investing in a Boom or Bust Market

Larry B. Loftis, Esq.

KAPLAN PUBLISHING

This publication is designed to provide accurate and authoritative information in regard to the subject matter covered. It is sold with the understanding that the publisher is not engaged in rendering legal, accounting, or other professional service. If legal advice or other expert assistance is required, the services of a competent professional should be sought.

Editorial Director: Jennifer Farthing
Development Editor: Joshua Martino
Senior Managing Editor, Production: Jack Kiburz
Production Artist: Todd Bowman
Cover Designer: DePinto Design

Published by Kaplan Publishing,
a division of Kaplan, Inc.

Printed in the United States of America

07 08 09 10 9 8 7 6 5 4 3 2 1

Library of Congress Cataloging-in-Publication Data

Loftis, Larry B.
    Successful real estate investing in a boom or bust market / Larry B. Loftis.
        p. cm.
    Includes bibliographical references and index.
    ISBN-13: 978-1-4195-9612-4
    ISBN-10: 1-4195-9612-8
    1. Real estate investment—United States. I. Title.
HD255.L65 2007
332.63'240973—dc22

                                                                2006101672

For information about ordering Kaplan Publishing books at special quantity discounts, please call 1-800-KAP-ITEM or write to Kaplan Publishing, 888 Seventh Ave., 22nd Floor, New York, NY 10106.

DEDICATION

This book is dedicated to Jim Seneff, one of the greatest real estate investors of our day, whose faith, balance, integrity, virtue, purpose, initiative, stewardship, and commitment to excellence inspire and instruct me daily.

Contents

Contents

One of the difficulties in the book publishing business is time delay. From the time a manuscript is begun, it may be nine months or longer before the book is distributed to retail sellers. When one writes a book about the real estate market, and how to buy in that market, nine months is an eternity. Prices can fluctuate considerably. Interest rates can change. Construction costs can rise.

As I write this in November of 2006, the real estate market has cooled, but remained remarkably stable. The real estate bulls are saying, "We told you so." The real estate bears are pointing to a few areas where prices have fallen 10 to 15 percent and are saying, "Just wait, the crash is still coming." No one has a crystal ball, including me. I cannot predict what the market will do in the future. What I can do, and the purpose of this book, is to reveal how to make real estate investing work in every market—boom, bust, or balanced. In that sense, my goal is for the book to be timeless.

Good real estate investors make money in every market, and the more dramatic the market swing, the more money they make. Having said that, remember that investors have different approaches to their investment strategies. Some investors prefer to "buy and hold," while others prefer to sell every two years or so. Still others like to time the market. That's the John D. Rockefeller approach: "Buy straw hats in winter." All of these strategies work, understanding the overall objectives. Unfortunately, many people don't use any strategy because they either don't know how or are too afraid.

I have friends who have said, "Man, I wish I invested in real estate at the beginning of the boom. I would have made a killing if I had just bought something in 2003 or early 2004." But back then they were too afraid to invest for fear of a real estate crash. They saw the early books and heard the early warning signs of an "overheated" real estate market, and they sat on their hands for fear of buying at the wrong time.

From what I've seen, most books on this topic simply predict that a real estate crash is coming. Maybe they are right; maybe they are wrong. At least one of these book authors has been wrong in the past on his predictions. So the timid souls lost tens of thousands of dollars, and possibly hundreds of thousands of dollars, sitting on the sidelines in the last boom market. Now they are afraid to go back out into the water. Maybe you are in that category. But what if you had a good idea of which way the market was going now? Would you get in the game? And what if you had workable strategies for every type of real estate market, boom or bust? Would you invest now?

You may have read about others who, like lemmings, just rushed headlong with the crowd, buying with reckless abandon. Many first-time investors bought condos in places such as Miami, never intending to live there or rehab the unit. They just figured that the rising tide lifts all ships and that the boom would never end. However, as Warren Buffett likes to say, "When the tide goes out, you see who has been swimming naked."

My purpose in writing this book was first to illustrate how to determine which type of market we are in—boom, bust, balanced, or a transition between them. It does make it easier to invest and make money if you can sail with the wind. This I have done in Chapter 1.

Second, I wanted to set the record straight on the danger of using historical statistics as a guide to the future. Statistics are helpful but may lead to incorrect conclusions, as we saw in 2002 when real estate bears predicted a crash on the crest of one of the biggest booms in U.S. history. In Chapter 2, I reveal how the plethora of real estate statistics coming at us every day can be paralyzing and lead to false conclusions. In Chapter 3, I give some background and statistical information (including myths) regarding how mortgage rates, inflation, and real estate cycles affect real estate prices.

My third goal with this book was to reveal solid strategies for investing in any type of market. To do that, however, I have to know investors' personal preferences in how they approach and buy real estate. In Chapters 4 and 5, I analyze the different approaches to real estate investing and selection of properties. For example, some buy only based on location, regardless of price. Others buy for cash flow. Others try to time the market. Once we know the investors' preferences, we can provide appropriate advice related to different markets (boom, bust, or balanced).

In Chapter 6, I detail the kind of property that is the safest during down or bust times, as well as where (in which city market) to invest. Naturally, I can't include every market in the country, but in Appendix A, I give appropriate investing information on 148 markets. In Chapters 7 and 8, I address strategies for investing in a balanced market (where we seem to be headed), and even another boom market, should we get to one in 2009 or 2010. In Chapter 9, I tell you where I think the market is heading.

Finally, in Chapter 10, I provide the latest available information from real estate organizations, companies, and economists on where the market is headed from now until 2010. This information should position you to take advantage of the changing markets over the next months and even years.

I hope that this book will give you the tools to invest in real estate now and in the near future. Find the strategy that fits your personality and objectives and stick with your plan. Remember also to always improve your properties. Real wealth is achieved by adding value. Ten years from now, you'll be glad you did.

Larry Loftis
November 2006

I would like to thank my editor, Vicki Smith, and my agent, Larry Jellen, for their tireless efforts on this project. Many thanks also to Jack Kiburz, my managing editor, who has provided his always professional guidance for three of my books now. I'd like to also thank Maureen McMahon, my publisher, for her commitment to me. Finally, I'd like to thank Dr. David Lereah of the National Association of REALTORS® for his assistance in tracking down a particular historical real estate statistic for me.

1

RECOGNIZING A BOOM, BUST, OR BALANCED MARKET

A crash in the real estate market is coming. Home prices have not only increased eightfold over the past 34 years, but have never declined in any single year. U.S. housing prices have increased 39 percent during the past 5 years. While the average home has appreciated over 25 percent in real terms after inflation since 1981, the underlying physical asset, ignoring tax advantages, has grown at more than double that rate. The chief economist at Morgan Stanley has warned that there is a very real danger of having the housing bubble burst. *Fortune* magazine reports that since 1996, U.S. real rents have increased just 10 percent, adjusted for inflation, one-third of the 30 percent jump in housing prices. In the past 3 years, the foreclosure rate has increased 25 percent. Nationally, 1.2 percent of all mortgages are in foreclosure. The number of personal bankruptcies is at an all-time high of 1.5 million a year. The number of houses that are sold each year before construction has even begun has increased in the past decade and is also at an all-time high. In more than 100 cities, real home prices have climbed twice as fast as household incomes since 1998. In the past 2 years, real national home prices have tripled the rate of growth of household incomes. An economist and former vice president at Goldman Sachs, now a visiting scholar at the Anderson School at UCLA, has stated: "The housing market is already starting to weaken. Many of the most overpriced metropolitan markets have begun to show weakened sales activity."[1]

Can anyone argue with these statistics? Can anyone argue that these statistics do *not* prove that a real estate crash is imminent? Indeed, I can. The reason I can challenge these statistics is because they were from 2002. In his 2003 release, *The Coming Crash in the Housing Market,* John Talbott made a compelling case that a crash in the real estate market was imminent. All of the statistics and quotes in the preceding paragraph are from his book.[2] Talbott is the economist making the quote in the last sentence. But if you followed his prediction and advice, you would have missed one of the largest "bull" housing markets in U.S. history.

Are the statistics in Talbott's book important? Of course. But, prognostication of real estate markets is much akin to fortune-telling. While the statistics may be significant, perhaps even startling, one should be very cautious about making wholesale changes to his or her real estate portfolio or investment strategy, even if it involves only the purchase of a first home. What Talbott and others don't tell you is that there is a very real risk of losing money in lost opportunity (what economists call "opportunity cost").

Many, many people made tens and hundreds of thousands of dollars by investing in real estate during this period. Others, heeding Talbott's warning, lost tens of thousands, and in many cases, hundreds of thousands of dollars, in lost opportunity cost dollars. If you had lived in San Diego, for example, and bought a house at the median price in October 2002, you would have paid $379,200. As of June 2006, the median price for a home in San Diego was $613,100.[3] If you decided not to buy that house due to the gloom and doom prognosticators, you would have lost $233,900 in equity.

In less than four years, you would have missed out on almost a quarter million dollars. Sadly, many who could have afforded a home in 2002 are now priced out of the market.

The good news, especially for those who may have missed the run-up in prices from 2002 to 2005, is that prices flattened in most markets in 2006 and are likely to take a further dip in 2007 in many, if not most, markets. Year 2007 likely will be a good time to buy again as prices find their floor.

As real estate bears have witnessed, the real estate market, like the U.S. economy, is extremely resilient. Betting against the United States is always risky business, statistics notwithstanding. Dr. Ravi Batra, who in the best-seller *Bankruptcy 1990* predicted the collapse of the American economy, was grossly wrong. In 1991, the late Larry Burkett, a respected financial advisor and radio host, wrote *The Coming Economic Earthquake*. Burkett predicted a meltdown of the American economy by 2000 or shortly thereafter due to the massive U.S. federal debt. Both authors made compelling cases with statistics. Both were wrong.

Having said that, one would be foolhardy to ignore the statistics pointed out by real estate bears. Likewise, while Batra and Burkett may have been wrong on the result of indicators such as the federal debt, their advice to carefully watch one's own debt and consumptive lifestyle was certainly proverbial. But the prudent real estate investor also should know that statistics alone will not cause a crash in the U.S. economy or the real estate market. We'll take a closer look at analyzing statistics in Chapter 2. Before doing so, let's consider what makes a boom, bust, or balanced real estate market.

BOOM, BUST, OR BALANCED MARKET

In any discussion of whether we are in for a boom or bust, we must know what is normal. What is the "average" market, against which we can measure deviations? Before answering that question, we must first remember four points largely ignored by real estate pundits and prognosticators:

1. There is no such thing as a "national" real estate market. Real estate is a local phenomenon.
2. We must segment whether we are speaking of single-family homes, residential multifamily, commercial, industrial property, or raw land.
3. Sales statistics almost never consider the improvement of properties.
4. Investment advice regarding boom or bust markets almost never considers the use or impact of leverage.

If we know national historical averages by category of real estate, we can then determine a norm, or baseline. Once we see the norm, we can begin to see whether the differences in appreciation, sales, time on the market, and other factors suggest a boom or bust, a buyer's market or seller's market. Let's now take a look at each type of market by real estate category.

SINGLE-FAMILY HOMES

Figure 1.1 shows the average and median price of single-family homes in the United States over a 30-year span (1975 to 2005). On a price analysis, the norm for appreciation of existing single-family homes is 6.7 percent annually (measured from 1968 to 2005), according to the National Association of REALTORS®. That figure may fluctuate rather dramatically by year or locale due to local economics, interest rates, job growth or losses, and net migration. As such, we might consider appreciation of 4 to 10 percent in any given year in the "normal" range.

A second indicator to consider for single-family homes is local sales. Are home sales increasing or decreasing? How long have

FIGURE 1.1 *U.S. House Prices Over the Past 30 Years*

July	Average Price	Median Price	July	Average Price	Median Price
1975	$ 42,300	$ 38,600	1991	$148,200	$120,000
1976	48,000	44,600	1992	137,700	118,000
1977	53,600	48,600	1993	143,400	123,900
1978	62,900	54,800	1994	144,400	124,400
1979	71,900	63,800	1995	154,200	131,000
1980	76,700	64,000	1996	168,400	144,200
1981	82,600	69,500	1997	175,500	145,900
1982	86,500	70,900	1998	179,800	149,900
1983	89,200	75,200	1999	189,100	158,200
1984	97,100	80,700	2000	202,200	169,000
1985	99,400	82,100	2001	209,300	175,000
1986	116,800	94,100	2002	217,800	175,600
1987	128,600	105,000	2003	248,400	190,200
1988	141,300	118,000	2004	279,200	212,400
1989	140,300	116,000	2005	275,000	215,000
1990	149,800	118,700			

Source: U.S. Census Bureau

they continued upward or downward? Have sales hit a record monthly high or low?

Tied closely to that is the number of listings on the multiple listing service (MLS) (if offered through a REALTOR®), the time it takes to sell the house, and the inventory of houses on the market (how long it will take the market to absorb the listings). Here's an example from my own market, Orlando. The historical norm for Orlando is about 6,000 listings (houses currently for sale on the MLS), a three- to six-month time frame to sell, and an inventory of six months' worth of homes. During the red-hot boom of 2005, however, MLS listings dropped to a historical low of only 2,000 homes. The inventory was only two months, and listings often were sold in days or weeks, often *above* the asking price.

FIGURE 1.2 *Identifying a Boom or Bust Market*

Market Type	Annual Price Appreciation	Time on the Market	Monthly Inventory of Homes
Boom	Over 12%	Days to weeks	Under 3 months
Strong	9–12%	Weeks to 3 months	3–5 months
Balanced	5–8%	3–6 months	5–7 months
Weak	1–4%	6–8 months	7–9 months
Bust	Under 1%	Over 8 months	Over 9 months

Clearly, those figures reveal a boom market. In September 2006, however, MLS listings for the Orlando market ballooned to over 28,700,[4] the inventory jumped to nine months, and owners counted on six months or more to sell their homes. While these figures are somewhat startling, the local real estate market did not crash. The market certainly cooled and some owners chose to reduce their asking price by 5 to 10 percent to move their properties. Others, however, held fast to their prices, and received them, by waiting longer. In fact, third-quarter prices for Orlando *increased* 3.7 percent from a year earlier.

If you wish to analyze what type of market you are in, or getting close to, consider these indicators: price, sales, and inventory. Figure 1.2 illustrates what your market might look like. The further the statistics move from the historical averages, the more your area is moving to a boom or bust market.

What Does a Boom Look Like?

While average appreciation is about 6.7 percent per year (1968 to 2005), the median U.S. home price jumped 83 percent between 1995 and 2005.[5] Let's also take a look at what a boom looks like in various areas of the country. If we take the years 2001 to 2005 as a boom period, notice the spectacular price increases in these areas:

Bakersfield, CA	171%
Fresno, CA	164%
Riverside, CA	157%
Modesto, CA	155%
Merced, CA	155%
Port St. Lucie, FL	153%
Miami, FL	150%
Los Angeles, CA	150%
Naples, FL	149%
Punta Gorda, FL	148%

Source: Fiserv Lending Solutions, Moody's Economy.com, and National Association of REALTORS®

Notice also that all of these areas of phenomenal price appreciation occurred in two states, California and Florida. These two states are typically the best for appreciation due to their warm climates and coastal locations. But remember that real estate is a local phenomenon. When one area is sizzling, another may be quite flat. Consider the overall appreciation of the following markets during the 2001 to 2005 boom years:

Burlington, NC	12%
Lafayette, IN	12%
Youngstown, OH	14%
Sioux City, IA	15%
Memphis, TN	15%
Kokomo, IN	16%
Victoria, TX	16%
Jonesboro, AR	16%
Canton, OH	16%
Springfield, OH	16%

Source: Money Magazine, Fiserv Lending Solutions, Moody's Economy.com

Just as California and Florida dominated the greatest appreciation markets, notice that Ohio and Indiana accounted for one-half of the bottom ten markets during this boom period. Houses in Lafayette, Indiana, and Burlington, North Carolina, appreciated at an annual rate of only 2.3 percent, while during the same period, the top ten markets saw an average annual gain of 20 percent.

Let's now look at a closer snapshot in time. In the year measured from the second quarter of 2005 to the second quarter of 2006, the Northeast saw an average price appreciation of 6.3 percent, while the Midwest saw a price *decline* of 2 percent.[6] In addition, while the South saw price appreciation of only 4.1 percent, notice the appreciation rates of the following Florida cities:

Ocala	25.3%
Gainesville	19.7%
Tampa/St. Petersburg/Clearwater	18.8%
Jacksonville	18.8%
Orlando	17.0%

Even less exciting cities such as Jackson, Mississippi; Montgomery, Alabama; Raleigh, North Carolina; Spartanburg, South Carolina; and Nashville, Tennessee, saw appreciation of over 11 percent (at 13.4, 13.1, 12.1, 11.5, and 11.4 percent, respectively). To assume that your real estate investments will track national, regional, or even state averages is foolish. Are you beginning to see that there is no *national* real estate market? In fact, markets within a state or even a city can vary considerably (see Appendix A for a complete list of appreciation rates for 148 markets).

What Does a Bust Look Like?

And just as prices in certain areas can go up while the surrounding areas are more stagnant, prices can sometimes decrease significantly (due to job losses, typically) while other markets

FIGURE 1.3 *Recent Real Estate Busts (Measured from Market Top to Bottom)*

City	Average Price Drop	Years	Years to Recover
Oklahoma City	−26.0%	1983–88	15
Austin	−25.8	1986–90	8
Houston	−22.0	1986–90	15
Los Angeles	−20.7	1990–96	10
Honolulu	−16.0	1994–99	9
Peoria	−15.4	1981–85	8
Detroit	−12.2	1981–84	6

Source: Local Market Monitor, CNNmoney.com

flourish. Take a look at recent busts in single-family residential markets in Figure 1.3.

Note, however, that during all of these markets, both the average and median prices for the country at large had decent, if not excellent, appreciation. Figure 1.4 shows the national average and median prices during the bust years for the selected markets shown in Figure 1.3.

Having said that, if you bought and sold a house between 1988 and 1994, during our recession and the first Gulf War, you would not have made much, if any, money on your house after factoring in real estate commissions and closing costs. That's assuming, of course, that you bought at fair market value and made no improvements to the property. But it's almost hard to lose money, even during recessionary times, if you buy property in a good location and hold it for five to eight years.

I bought my first house in 1989, the worst time to be buying. Prices were fairly flat from 1989 until 1994. I sold in 1996, just as prices began to take off. I bought at $87,500 and sold for $126,500. Because I was in a good location, I received enough street traffic to sell it without a broker. As such, even buying and selling at almost the worst times, I still made $39,000, less closing

FIGURE 1.4 *National Average and Median Price during Bust Years*

Years	U.S. Average Price	U.S. Median Price
1981–1985		
1981	$82,600	$69,500
1985	99,400	82,100
1983–1988		
1983	89,200	75,200
1988	141,300	118,000
1986–1990		
1986	116,800	94,100
1990	149,800	118,700
1990–1996		
1990	149,800	118,700
1996	168,400	144,200
1994–1999		
1994	144,400	124,400
1999	189,100	158,200

costs. Remember also that I had paid my mortgage down during this time and received tremendous tax benefits. If I knew then what I know now, I would have bought that house (or another) at least 10 percent under market and made improvements. Had I done so, I would have made at least $50,000 in one of our worst real estate markets.

RESIDENTIAL MULTIFAMILY

Residential multifamily refers to investment properties of two to four units—duplexes, triplexes, and quads. These properties are tracked, and valued, not by price per se, but by the *gross rent multiplier,* or GRM. The GRM is a way to compare the income-producing value of a property relative to its price. To determine the GRM of a property, divide the purchase price by the gross annual rents. For example, if you were to purchase a triplex for $300,000 and the property brought in $2,000 per month, or $24,000 annually, your GRM would be 12.5.

$$GRM = \text{Purchase price} \div \text{Annual rents}$$
$$\$300,000 \div \$24,000 = 12.5$$

This valuation method is *the* essential valuation tool used when investing in residential multifamily units. In my prior book, *Investing in Duplexes, Triplexes, and Quads: The Fastest and Safest Way to Real Estate Wealth* (Kaplan, 2006), I go into great detail on how to use the GRM. In this type of property, it's the GRM that will tell you whether you'll be receiving positive or negative cash flow. For our purposes here, it will also assist in telling us whether the market is heading in a boom or bust direction. Keep in mind, of course, that the quality and location of a property also influence its GRM (because these factors affect the rents that can be charged). Figure 1.5 illustrates how to use GRM to analyze your residential multifamily market.

When I bought a quad in an upscale part of downtown Orlando in 2004, I purchased the property at a GRM of 13.5. I thought it

FIGURE 1.5 *Using GRM to Analyze Residential Multifamily Properties*

Market Type	GRM	Cash Flow
Boom	Over 16	Major negative cash flow
Seller's Market	12–16	Slight negative cash flow
Balanced	8–11	Breakeven
Buyer's Market	5–7	Slight positive cash flow
Bust	Under 5	Major positive cash flow

was an outrageous price and GRM at the time but I knew that the area was hot and getting hotter. It was the "cool" place to be. By the fall of 2005, you couldn't touch any multifamily properties in this area for a GRM under 18. Many were listed at over 20. In December 2005, I made a list of every duplex, triplex, and quad within two zip codes in downtown Orlando. The GRM ranged from 16 on the fringe of downtown, to 44 in the heart of downtown. I bought the property with the 16 GRM (purchased at a 15.5 GRM), a triplex, in December 2005. As I write this in the late fall of 2006, the GRM for sold properties has been in the range of 13.5 to 22, the real estate slowdown notwithstanding. Many current listings are in the low to mid-20s. At the beach where I own another property, I saw a quad for sale today listed for a GRM of 30. And it's not even oceanfront property. You've heard it before: location, location, location.

As these numbers reveal, one category of real estate may be appreciating while another is depreciating. Here's why. As houses become less affordable due to the recent real estate boom, more people are forced to continue renting an apartment. In turn, you have more renters chasing fewer available apartments. Add to that the recent frenzy of apartment complexes converting into condos and you have still fewer apartments available. This drives up rents, which drives up a property's annual income, which increases the property's value and ultimate sales price. So while single-family homes may see a decrease in average sales price, multifamily properties could see an average price increase(including vacant land zoned as such).

COMMERCIAL

Commercial property consists of residential multifamily properties of five or more units, office, retail, shopping centers, and industrial properties. Just as single-family properties could be

FIGURE 1.6 *Range of Cap Rates*

Market	Cap Rates
Boom	3–6
Seller's Market	7–8
Balanced	9–11
Buyer's Market	12–13
Bust	13+

decreasing in price while apartments are increasing in price, commercial properties are also independent in nature and may fluctuate in price. For example, single-family residential properties might be setting record sales and have tremendous price appreciation while the commercial property market is flat. As such, we must analyze the commercial property on its own merit by looking at capitalization rates. A cap rate is the net operating income (NOI) of a property divided by the sales price. This calculation is how a commercial property is valued.

$$\text{Cap rate} = \text{Net operating income} \div \text{Sales price}$$

For example, a million-dollar property generating $100,000 in net income each year would have a cap rate of 10 percent. The higher the cap rate, the better the bargain for the buyer. The lower the cap rate, the better the bargain for the seller. Figure 1.6 illustrates the range of cap rates for each market type.

Keep in mind that many factors affect cap rates. In Florida, for example, many apartment complexes are currently being converted into condos. Due to this frenzy, investors have not paid much attention to the property's NOI because the buyers are not going to run the property as an apartment complex. Instead, they are buying these apartments, perhaps doing some light rehab, and then converting the units to condos and selling them for top

FIGURE 1.7 *Market Type Indicators*

	Boom	Seller's Market	Balanced	Buyer's Market	Bust
Interest Rates	Very Low (5–7%)	Low (7–8%)	Medium (8–9%)	High (9–11%)	High (11+%)
Prices	Very High	High	Medium	Low	Very Low
	GRM Cap Over 16 3–6	GRM Cap 12–16 7–8	GRM Cap 8–11 9–11	GRM Cap 5–7 12–13	GRM Cap Under 5 13+
Appreciation	High 10+%	Medium to High 8–9%	Medium 5–8%	Medium to Low 3–5%	Low Under 3%
Cash Flow	Major Negative	Slight Negative	Breakeven to Positive	Slight Positive	Major Positive

dollar. In 2005 and 2006, for example, the going rate for large complexes was a cap rate of only 3 percent. Virtually all of the sales were conversions. When the frenzy curtails, cap rates will return to more historic levels.

Take a look at Figure 1.7. This chart will give you an overview of all of the indicators suggesting a market type. Analyze all of this information according to your property type (i.e., single-family home, residential multifamily, or commercial) and locality.

MONEY MADE IN THE TRANSITIONS

In real estate, money is made by adding value (i.e., improvements or new use), increasing rents, and buying and selling in the transitions between markets. For example, those investors who bought properties in the years 2001 and 2002 bought in a transition from a buyer's market to a boom. By 2003, the boom was under way. In 2004 and 2005, property owners saw their properties skyrocket in value. Those who purchased single-family homes in strong markets in 2001 and 2002 and sold them in 2005, the peak of the boom, made a killing.

Year 2006 has proven to be a transition from the boom to a buyer's market again. Some would call it a correction, and others would call it the crest of a bust. The question, of course, is what is in store for 2007? Will it prove to be the transition from a buyer's market back to a balanced or seller's market? Or will the slide continue into a full-fledged bust? In either case, savvy real estate investors will be making money all the way through as they take what the market gives them. In this book, I hope to give you enough information to help you determine which way your own market is heading, and how to make money in it.

2

STATISTICS LIE

There are three kinds of commonly recognized untruths:
Lies, damn lies, and statistics.

Mark Twain

Thomas Carlyle, the Scottish writer and philosopher, once opined, "Statistics are the greatest liars of them all." Have you ever noticed studies, polls, and reports that seemed incredulous? Most often, statistics are given to influence a reader or consumer. Rarely does the statistician or pollster reveal his or her inherent biases, assumptions, or limited scope of research. In many cases, the writer has an undisclosed conflict of interest. These influencing factors often sway statistics to support the writer, even though other studies or broader research might suggest just the opposite conclusion.

Real estate research is not immune from such improper statistical influences. In analyzing real estate markets, always consider the following six factors when reviewing reports, articles, and predictions:

1. Story versus research
2. National versus local market
3. Conflict of interest

4. Conflict of statistics
5. The danger of using statistics to predict the future
6. The elephant in the living room

STORY VERSUS RESEARCH

On September 25, 2006, the homepage on CNNmoney.com ran this story headline: **Help! Home for sale—Young and Ballanco: The Orlando-based couple thought they were in a bubble. Are they in a bust?** When I saw this title I was a bit skeptical because, living in Orlando, I knew the market remained strong and that sellers were still getting very close to their asking prices. The article began:

When Casey Young and his wife Jaime Ballanco put their Orlando house on the market back in March, they had no clue that the property would not sell. As far as they were concerned, Orlando was still bubbling. After all, home prices were supposedly growing in the neighborhood of 20 percent a year. But what the top-line statistics masked was that a slowdown was already underway—from the fourth quarter of 2005 to the first quarter of 2006, the median home price in Orlando fell 0.5 percent.

In short, the article gave the impression that Orlando, like other markets, had succumbed to the real estate slowdown and might "bust." The article correctly reported that the number of homes on the market in Orange and Seminole counties had skyrocketed, from 4,473 in July 2005 to 19,827 in July 2006. However, the article also revealed a clear attempt to create an emotional story:

"We're planning on starting a family someday," says the 30-year-old Young, who builds simulation software for a defense contractor. "We wanted a bigger home—with a pool."

The new house cost $562,000 so they were really counting on profits from the old place to help. They had bought their current four-bedroom, two-and-a-half-bath, 2,861-square-foot contemporary new on the last day of 2002, paying $167,000.

Doesn't it seem unusual that such a young couple would be seeking a $562,000 house? And here's the emotional appeal:

To know the problem is no consolation to the couple, who are increasingly feeling the stress. They have to make a decision soon about whether to go ahead with the purchase and hope they'll sell the old house, or give up the new place and lose their $28,000 deposit.

They're due to close Oct. 24.

"I absolutely need the profit from my old home to afford the new one," says Young. "Even with rental income from one of the homes, there's no way I can afford both mortgages at the same time."

Do you feel their pain? "Stress," "lose their $28,000 deposit," "due to close Oct. 24," "no way I can afford both mortgages"—these phrases suggest this young couple might lose $28,000 and the house they *need* for their family. But this story didn't seem to mesh with my knowledge of the stable Orlando real estate market. So I looked closer at the article and the cause of the couple's problem.

First, the couple listed the house for sale in March 2006 for $402,000. They purchased it on December 31, 2002, for $167,000. Notwithstanding some minor improvements by the couple, doesn't it seem a bit unusual to expect appreciation of $235,000 in only 45 months?

Second, the article revealed one "improvement," a koi pond, and included a photo. Looking at the photo, my first reaction was to think about how much it would cost to get rid of this "improvement." It looked awful. A polite real estate agent might describe it as an "owner specific" improvement. That addition certainly added to the couple's delay in selling the home.

The article listed the REALTOR® hired to sell the house; the same REALTOR® I hired to sell my personal residence a few years ago. I suspect that the REALTOR®, who is exceedingly polite and nice, diplomatically convinced the couple to lower the price. The article stated that the price was lowered to $369,000, and then to $349,000. Looking at the photo of the house, it appears to remain overpriced. It's no wonder that the house hasn't sold. Rather than suffering from a real estate bust, this couple seems to have misjudged the value of their home.

On October 5, 2006, less than a month after this article appeared on CNNmoney.com, the *Orlando Sentinel* ran a front page feature entitled: **Report: Area's housing prices won't plunge: Declines locally will be slim to none and may have occurred already, experts say.** So much for the notion of an Orlando real estate bust. The CNNmoney.com article was a story. The *Orlando Sentinel* article revealed more telling research. While research statistics can be highly misleading, they certainly take precedence over a story. Beware of stories disguised as research, and carefully scrutinize research and studies. Trust your instincts if you know the local market.

The *Orlando Sentinel* article revealed that Moody's Economy.com conducted a study of 379 U.S. metropolitan areas and concluded that only 133 of the markets would experience slumps during 2006 or during the next one to four years. Of these 133 markets, over 20 markets were expected to "crash." A crash was defined as a decline in median price of 10 percent or more. Here again, we have to be discerning. Can you see the problem? The study has defined a term for us. A crash is defined as a drop in median price of 10 percent or more. But that's not how the stock market is viewed. The last stock market crash was on Black Monday, October 19, 1987, when the Dow Jones Industrial Average lost 22.6 percent of its value in one day.

We could certainly debate whether the cities in the Moody's Economy.com study will crash. Using the stock market as a guide, one might conclude that no real estate market will crash. The worst area, Danville, Illinois, is expected to see a decline of 18.7 percent, according to the study.

Ironically, here's what the article did *not* say, but could have: "The study reveals that two-thirds of U.S. real estate markets will remain stable over the next four years." Or, the article could have said this: "The study shows that only 7 percent of U.S. real estate markets will see declines of 10 to 19 percent." See how statistics work? It all depends on the writer's perspective.

NATIONAL VERSUS LOCAL MARKET

Most articles that discuss real estate boom or bust markets limit their research and statistics to national averages. But real estate is a local phenomenon. How can you compare housing prices in San Francisco, one of the hottest markets in the country, with Des Moines? How can you compare popular coastal cities such as Miami or Naples with Tulsa? You can't. In fact, you can't even compare cities in the same state. Miami, Orlando, and Panama City might have completely different markets. The same is true for Dallas, Houston, and San Antonio, or Los Angeles, Fresno, and Stockton.

Even parts of the same city can have very different markets. I can tell you areas of metropolitan Orlando that will get phenomenal appreciation, and other areas 15 minutes away that will get poor appreciation. So any study analyzing real estate nationally will skew the numbers for both the big or hot cities (e.g., New York City, San Francisco, Los Angeles, San Diego, Miami, Palm Beach,

Naples, Sarasota) as well as the smaller, less popular cities such as Des Moines, Tulsa, or Corpus Christi.

For example, notice the appreciation rates of the hottest markets from 2001 to 2005:

Bakersfield, CA	171%
Fresno, CA	164%
Riverside, CA	157%
Modesto, CA	155%
Merced, CA	155%
Port St. Lucie, FL	153%
Miami, FL	150%
Los Angeles, CA	150%
Naples, FL	149%
Punta Gorda, FL	148%

Source: *Money* Magazine, Fiserv Lending Solutions, Moody's Economy.com

Now during this same time, notice the appreciation rates of the weakest markets from 2001 to 2005:

Burlington, NC	12%
Lafayette, IN	12%
Youngstown, OH	14%
Sioux City, IA	15%
Memphis, TN	15%
Kokomo, IN	16%
Victoria, TX	16%
Jonesboro, AR	16%
Canton, OH	16%
Springfield, OH	16%

Source: *Money* Magazine, Fiserv Lending Solutions, Moody's Economy.com

If you were considering buying a home in Canton, Ohio, with a four-year appreciation of only 16 percent, you probably wouldn't take into consideration the national appreciation average, which would be skewed by the California and Florida appreciation rates. In short, there's no such thing as a national real estate market. Any reports of national figures may help you with the overall economy and big picture, but you better be looking more carefully at what is going on in that local market.

CONFLICT OF INTEREST

In any discussion of reports, trends, and statistics, the careful consumer always asks whether the author or reporter has a conflict of interest or inherent bias. David Lereah, chief economist for the National Association of REALTORS® (NAR), released a 2005 book entitled, *Are You Missing the Real Estate Boom?* Lereah has received severe criticism for suggesting a stable real estate market due to his potential conflict of interest. Indeed, the critics are wise to note that Lereah may have a potential conflict of interest. However, the astute reader must ask these questions:

- Does Lereah's conflict, or potential conflict, invalidate his conclusions? The answer, of course, is not necessarily. Lereah may prove to be accurate in his research and conclusions, conflict notwithstanding.
- Do the critics have their own conflicts of interest? Are their conclusions driven by a desire to sell books and gain financially? Chances are, Lereah is paid an annual salary from the NAR, while real estate authors critical of Lereah are paid a commission (royalties, to be specific) on how many books they can sell. The more alarming their conclusions, the more books they sell, and the more money they make.

This reminds me of Dr. Ravi Batra, whose book, *Bankruptcy 1990,* sold well but his predictions were inaccurate.

- Does the author have experience in the field for which he is making predictions, and how accurate has he been in the past? For example, John Talbott claims no experience in real estate investing, yet presupposes that academics (like himself) are more equipped to provide predictions for real estate. Talbott's predictions in 2006, however, are mollified by the severity of his inaccurate predictions in his 2003 book, *The Coming Crash in the Housing Market.*

The astute reader notes potential conflicts of interest and other mollifying qualifications, but doesn't necessarily reject the expert's research or conclusions. In our case, valuable information can be gleaned from Lereah, Talbott, and other pundits. However, we should use the aggregate information and determine our own conclusions, recognizing potential conflicts, limited research (i.e., national versus local), limitations of expertise, and so on.

CONFLICT OF STATISTICS

Have you ever noticed that some experts reach different conclusions while using the same statistics? We know that existing home prices have been escalating at a clip of about 6.7 percent (according to the NAR) for the past 37 years. Prices now seem unthinkable compared to prices just 10 years ago due to historic increases from 2003 to 2005. But some academics suggest that prices really have been flat up until our current boom.

For example, John Talbott cites research by Yale University's Robert Shiller, claiming that house prices have been flat for 100 years prior to 1996. They are referring to "real" prices, as adjusted for inflation. In *Sell Now!,* Talbott shows a graph prepared by Shiller suggesting that real prices of homes were higher in 1955 than in

1995.[1] I understand basic economics and prices as adjusted for inflation, but this suggestion seems hard to believe. I don't know the exact figures for house prices and inflation from 1955 to 1963, when the U.S. Census Bureau began tracking house prices, but I have to be a bit skeptical about Shiller's conclusions. Consider, for example, the Census Bureau's figures for existing home sales for these years:

Year (Quarter)	Median Price
1963 (Q1)	$ 17,200
1995 (Q1)	$127,900

The Census Bureau numbers are in nominal or face value prices, while Shiller is comparing inflation-adjusted numbers. However, notwithstanding adjustments for inflation, it seems hard to believe a house in 1955 would have a higher real value than one in 1995. Perhaps technically, Shiller is correct. But I, and other real estate investors, work with the brick and mortar of real properties, not inflation-adjusted statistics. Somehow I think the investor who purchased a house for $17,200 in 1963 believes his 1995 value of $127,900 represents a wonderful return on investment (not to mention the 2005 median price of $222,310), inflation notwithstanding.

At the very least, when one compares sales prices, one must always define terms. Are we looking at average or median prices (i.e., one-half sold above this figure and one-half sold below this figure), or nominal or "real" (inflation-adjusted) prices? If we are looking at inflation-adjusted prices, whose figure for inflation are we using? In most cases, experts giving inflation-adjusted prices do not reveal the average inflation rate that they are using. Few ask the question, "Is this inflation figure used for the analysis correct?" Once we understand the terms used, and the adjustments made (whether appropriate or inappropriate), we can see why experts sometimes seem to give contradictory conclusions while dealing with the same raw data.

THE DANGER OF USING STATISTICS TO PREDICT THE FUTURE

At the beginning of Chapter 1, I quoted several statistics used by John Talbott in *The Coming Crash in the Housing Market*. These statistics seemed to be accurate, compelling, and startling. Talbott's call for an immediate real estate crash seemed logical at the time. But Talbott was wrong on the timing, and appears to be wrong on the occurrence of a crash at all. Talbott writes in 2003: "The housing market is already starting to weaken. Many of the most overpriced metropolitan markets have begun to show weakened sales activity."[2] Citing a financial analyst at an investment bank (with no apparent real estate experience), Talbott writes, "In places like Manhattan and San Francisco, prices could easily drop 40 or 50 percent."[3]

Using legitimate and compelling statistics, Talbott was wrong. Grossly wrong. Talbott cites the average October 2002 price of a home in San Francisco as $530,900.[4] Did that market crash by losing 40 to 50 percent of its value? No. Did it crash by losing 25 percent of its value? No. Did it weaken? No. Did it cool? No. As of the second quarter of 2006, the average price of a San Francisco home had jumped to $752,000. If a homeowner followed Talbott's predictions and sold his San Francisco home in late 2002 or early 2003, he would have lost $221,000 in equity gain.

And Talbott's misjudgment was not limited to San Francisco. Talbott's book also included a table titled, "Housing Price Analysis by Major Metropolitan Area," in which markets were ranked by house prices as a multiple of income. Talbott warns:

> I would focus your attention in Table 6.3 to those areas of the country that have average multiples above 3.0. These are the areas of highest risk should there be a price decline. Not only are these the priciest with the highest room to fall, but they would also be expected to have the most number

of highly indebted homeowners. As the worst cases begin
to fail, and the banks foreclose and dump them on the
market, all prices suffer.[5]

In short, Talbott is saying that the greater the city's multiple of
income ratio, the greater the risk. San Diego and San Francisco,
then, would be the riskiest markets in the country with multiples
of income over 6. His reference of 3.0 as a particular warning
threshold would cover the top 30 markets in his analysis. Figure
2.1 summarizes the pertinent numbers from Talbott's Table 6.3
for the top 30 markets.[6]

Talbott's assessment that the markets with the least affordable
houses would be at most risk for a dramatic price decline seems
reasonable. After all, if potential buyers cannot afford a house,
how can the prices continue to climb? So how did Talbott fare
in his predictions? His numbers shown in Figure 2.1 were as of
October 2002. Let's see what happened in each market as of the
second quarter of 2006. Figure 2.2 adds the 2006 median price
next to Talbott's chart.

Recall that these 30 markets are the *riskiest* markets for a soft
or weak real estate market, according to Talbott's analysis (and
the analysis of others) of price to market area income. According to this formula, these markets should have declined dramatically during the 2006 real estate slump. But take a careful look at
the numbers in Figure 2.2. *Not one* of these markets declined in
median price from their October 2002 figure. On the contrary,
every market median price increased. Many markets saw increases
of $100,00 or more. Some market median prices doubled—in less
than four years.

Similarly, John Rubino, in his 2003 release, *How to Profit from
the Coming Real Estate Bust,* was wildly inaccurate in his predictions.
Suggesting a recession in 2004, one of the greatest real estate
boom years in U.S. history, Rubino wrote:

FIGURE 2.1 *Top 30 Markets as of October 2002*

Ranking by Multiple	Metropolitan Area	Housing Price October 2002	Multiple of Income
1	San Diego, CA	$379,200	6.31
2	San Francisco Bay Area, CA	530,900	6.17
3	Orange County, CA	439,400	5.81
4	Boston, MA	415,800	5.60
5	Honolulu, HI	345,000	5.51
6	Los Angeles Area, CA	290,000	5.26
7	Bergen/Passaic, NJ	351,000	4.45
8	Newark, NJ	326,200	4.14
9	Miami/Hialeah, FL	198,800	4.12
10	New York/Long Island, NY	328,000	4.02
11	Nassau/Suffolk, NY	326,200	3.93
12	Monmouth/Ocean, NJ	273,500	3.91
13	Sacramento, CA	219,800	3.84
14	Providence, RI	203,300	3.76
15	Riverside/San Bernardino, CA	181,000	3.60
16	Ft. Lauderdale/Hollywood/Pompano, FL	205,500	3.41
17	Seattle, WA	261,500	3.36
18	Sarasota, FL	178,500	3.34
19	Denver, CO	233,600	3.34
20	Tacoma, WA	173,600	3.34
21	Charleston, SC	164,000	3.33
22	Eugene/Springfield, OR	145,200	3.32
23	Portland, ME	178,500	3.31
24	Middlesex/Somerset/Hunterdon, NJ	296,300	3.29
25	Portland, OR	182,700	3.19
26	Colorado Springs, CO	175,500	3.09
27	Chicago, IL	230,200	3.05
28	New Haven/Meriden, CT	199,200	3.05
29	Las Vegas, NV	163,200	3.01
30	Tucson, AZ	147,600	3.00

FIGURE 2.2 *Comparison of Housing Prices from October 2002 to June 2006*

Ranking by Multiple	Metropolitan Area	Housing Price October 2002	Multiple of Income	Housing Price June 2006*
1	San Diego, CA	$379,200	6.31	$613,100
2	San Francisco Bay Area, CA	530,900	6.17	$751,900
3	Orange County, CA	439,400	5.81	$726,200
4	Boston, MA	415,800	5.60	unavailable
5	Honolulu, HI	345,000	5.51	$640,000
6	Los Angeles Area, CA	290,000	5.26	$576,300
7	Bergen/Passaic, NJ	351,000	4.45	unavailable
8	Newark, NJ	326,200	4.14	$443,800
9	Miami/Hialeah, FL	198,800	4.12	$376,200**
10	New York/Long Island, NY	328,000	4.02	$473,700
11	Nassau/Suffolk, NY	326,200	3.93	$478,000
12	Monmouth/Ocean, NJ	273,500	3.91	unavailable
13	Sacramento, CA	219,800	3.84	$380,600
14	Providence, RI	203,300	3.76	$291,100
15	Riverside/San Bernardino, CA	181,000	3.60	$395,700
16	Ft. Lauderdale/Hollywood/Pompano, FL	205,500	3.41	$376,200**
17	Seattle, WA	261,500	3.36	unavailable
18	Sarasota, FL	178,500	3.34	$350,900
19	Denver, CO	233,600	3.34	$255,200
20	Tacoma, WA	173,600	3.34	unavailable
21	Charleston, SC	164,000	3.33	$213,800
22	Eugene/Springfield, OR	145,200	3.32	$227,600
23	Portland, ME	178,500	3.31	$242,700
24	Middlesex/Somerset/Hunterdon, NJ	296,300	3.29	unavailable
25	Portland, OR	182,700	3.19	$283,400
26	Colorado Springs, CO	175,500	3.09	$218,300
27	Chicago, IL	230,200	3.05	$278,500
28	New Haven/Meriden, CT	199,200	3.05	$292,600
29	Las Vegas, NV	163,200	3.01	$319,100
30	Tucson, AZ	147,600	3.00	$247,300

* National Association of REALTORS®
** NAR combined the Miami and Ft. Lauderdale markets

So the question today [2003] is not just whether home prices in Boston and San Francisco will fall by 30 percent over the next few years . . . but whether the bursting of the housing bubble will deflate the rest of the economy. . . . This self-reinforcing cycle ends only when the people who didn't leverage themselves to the hilt start buying up foreclosed homes and busted home builder stocks for pennies on the 2002 dollar. In short, we'll get the recession we should have had in 2001, but three years later, in 2004. And this is the optimistic scenario.[7]

Ironically enough, as I write this section on October 11, 2006, the lead article on the business page of my local paper, the *Orlando Sentinel,* states: **Home builders may be turning corner: Wall Street analysts upgrade companies' stock.** Rather than being able to buy homebuilder stocks for pennies on the dollar, as Rubino predicted, investors likely will find no major bargains in homebuilder stocks. Analysts at JP Morgan Securities upgraded stocks on national builders such as D.R. Horton, Standard Pacific Corp., and Toll Brothers on grounds that the worst of the slump may be over.

THE ELEPHANT IN THE LIVING ROOM

Within the latest few years a number of books have been released advising consumers on how to invest in the upcoming real estate crash. Most of the books reveal compelling statistics to make their case. But there's an elephant in the living room. Can you see it? Most of the authors giving real estate advice for the upcoming crash are not real estate investors.[8] Most are economists, academics, or investment bankers. Would you trust your stock portfolio to a manager who does not personally invest in stocks? You must ask the same question about following real estate advice from one who does not personally invest in real estate. Again, their lack of

real estate experience does not necessarily invalidate their conclusions. However, because they are not involved real estate, they
likely will have few options for how to implement strategies to deal
with their conclusions. For example, none of the crash books that
I've seen analyze the safety net of making improvements, focus on
the significance of the GRM and cap rates, or offer the strategies
of long-term buy and hold, refinancing, and/or pyramiding.

In Talbott's *The Coming Crash in the Housing Market,* for example,
he cites research by his colleague at the UCLA Anderson School
of Management, Professor Ed Leamer. Using the stock market as a
guide, Leamer and Talbott analyze the P/E (price-earnings ratio)
of housing. In the stock market, a stock can be valued by taking
its price and dividing by the per share earnings of the company.
Talbott says of Leamer's analysis: "[W]hen people talk about how
expensive stocks are they talk about how high their P/Es are. Similarly, Professor Leamer asks what housing P/E we are paying for
our homes. His definition of a housing P/E is its market price
divided by the annual rental income it could generate."[9] Surpris-
ingly, Professor Leamer and Talbott apparently do not realize
that real estate investors have used this very analysis for decades;
it's called the GRM, or *gross rent multiplier.* Almost all multifamily
real estate investors are aware of this valuation method. Virtually
every commercial real estate broker and appraiser in the country
is aware of this term.

And here's where academics reveal their limitations. Because
they are not real estate investors, they cannot give specific advice
on what normal or acceptable GRM (or "housing P/E ratio," as
Leamer calls it) rates would be. On October 10, 2006, for example,
Bloomberg.com estimated the P/E of Boeing, one of the 30 blue
chip stocks included in the Dow Jones Industrial Average, at 35. Is
that about right for investment real estate? Talbott doesn't address
the issue in his books. (To see acceptable GRM rates, review Figure 1.5 in Chapter 1.)

In addition, the economist advisors generally don't address the microeconomics of local markets, where the real estate investing is occurring. More importantly, however, is the fact that these advisors don't address *investing* at all. Their main approach is only to address *buying*. What's the difference? A buyer buys a house in which to live. An investor buys a house from which to make money. A buyer only buys single-family residences. An investor buys land, condos, houses, duplexes, triplexes, quads, apartments, strip malls, shopping centers, office buildings, and industrial buildings. A buyer pays full fair market value. An investor typically buys at 50 to 95 cents on the dollar. A buyer rarely makes immediate improvements. An investor makes immediate improvements to increase rents and property value.

DO STATISTICS REALLY MATTER TO THE INVESTOR?

Ironically, these economist prognosticators (and all of the "crash" authors that I've seen) are writing books for single-family homebuyers, not investors. The books and statistics related to the boom or expected crash only address single-family homes and generally don't mention strategies for buying at a discount, improving the property, increasing rents (or renting at all, for that matter), valuing properties with the GRM or cap rates, or financing options. But most single-family homebuyers generally have little concern for markets, trends, and statistics. These buyers are concerned about having enough square feet to comfortably house their families, the quality of the local schools, the location, and the general appearance of the house. These buyers are not looking to make money on their homes, per se. As such, the crash books, written primarily about single-family properties, have little relevance to their main audience, the average family homebuyer.

The real estate investor, on the other hand, desires to make money in ever-changing markets. But most real estate investors buy multifamily or commercial properties, not single-family homes. Sure, many real estate investors are "flippers," meaning they buy a house, fix it up, and immediately put it back on the market for a quick profit. But one- or two-year trends have little significance for the flipper. He or she intends to be in and out of the market within six months.

And so the crash books would appear to be written for real estate investors, yet they don't address the investors' primary properties—multifamily and commercial—or those involved with flipping single-family homes. And because most of the economist writers are not real estate investors, they cannot give specific advice on buying properties under fair market value (whether that be pre-crash or post-crash) or making improvements to increase the value of the property. Hopefully, this book will bridge that gap for the real estate investor.

3

REAL ESTATE ECONOMICS 101

*Real estate statistics are almost always for the
single-family homeowner, not the investor.*

In the last chapter, we saw that statistics can be misleading. Statistics, particularly involving mortgage rates, inflation rates, prices, and real estate cycles, can also be paralyzing. Certainly a real estate investor would want to keep track of mortgage rates, unemployment, the economy, and supply and demand (determined, in part, by new development). But let's take a look at four statistics—interest rates, single-family home prices, inflation, and real estate cycles—that many follow closely before investing in real estate.

INTEREST RATES AND SINGLE-FAMILY HOME PRICES

Interest rates are often thought to highly influence prices and values of real estate. The thinking goes, as interest rates rise, mortgage payments become higher and harder to make. As a real estate investor, it becomes harder to reach positive cash flow as interest rates rise. The contemplated result is that property prices decrease in value because fewer investors are interested. These investors receive lower returns on their money, or lose money, as interest rates climb.

Let's look at a simple example. Assume that you had $50,000 on hand to put down on a real estate purchase. The type of real estate doesn't really matter for our example, but let's assume that you are putting 20 percent down (generally required on investor properties). As such, you can buy a $250,000 property. That would leave you with a loan amount of $200,000. If we are talking about residential property, you can amortize that loan over 30 years (typically 20 to 25 years for commercial property). If our interest rate is 7 percent, our mortgage payment of principal and interest is $1,330.60 per month. But notice what happens at each percent increase in the rate:

Interest Rate	Payment
7%	$1,330.60
8%	$1,467.53
9%	$1,609.25
10%	$1,755.14
11%	$1,904.65
12%	$2,057.23

Notice that your mortgage payment has increased over $700 per month as we moved from 7 to 12 percent interest. If this is a rental house, duplex, triplex, or quad, chances are that you would move from positive cash flow to negative cash flow.

If you are under 30, you may think that an interest rate of 11 or 12 percent is preposterous. But I bought my first house at 11 percent, the going rate, in 1989. We live in the luxury now of some of the lowest rates in recent history. Take a look at the interest rates over the past 34 years in Figure 3.1.

Notice that for 12 years, from 1979 to 1990, interest rates were over 10 percent. Notice that for 14 years, from 1978 to 1991, they

FIGURE 3.1 *30-Year Average Mortgage Rate Since 1972*

Year	30-Year Rate	Year	30-Year Rate
1972	7.38%	1990	10.13%
1973	8.09	1991	9.23
1974	9.19	1992	8.40
1975	9.04	1993	7.33
1976	8.86	1994	8.36
1977	8.84	1995	7.96
1978	9.63	1996	7.81
1979	11.19	1997	7.60
1980	13.77	1998	6.94
1981	16.63	1999	7.43
1982	16.08	2000	8.06
1983	13.23	2001	6.97
1984	13.87	2002	6.54
1985	12.42	2003	5.82
1986	10.18	2004	5.84
1987	10.20	2005	5.87
1988	10.34	2006*	6.36
1989	10.32		

* Rate as of October 19, 2006

were over 9 percent. What do you think happened to prices for single-family homes during these years? They went down or were flat, right? Wrong. Take a look at our history of single-family home prices in Figure 3.2 and compare with these interest rates.

You would think that prices would be flat or go down during these years. However, they gradually climbed year after year, with a slump only from 1988 to 1992. In 1979, interest rates were over 11 percent. From 1980 to 1984, rates were over 13 percent. But during this five-year span, the median single-family home price increased from $63,800 to $80,700, while the average price jumped from $71,900 to $97,100. Even when rates were at an

FIGURE 3.2 *Single-Family Home Prices Over the Past 30 Years*

July	Average Price	Median Price	30-Year Rate
1975	$ 42,300	$ 38,600	9.04%
1976	48,000	44,600	8.86
1977	53,600	48,600	8.84
1978	62,900	54,800	9.63
1979	71,900	63,800	11.19
1980	76,700	64,000	13.77
1981	82,600	69,500	16.63
1982	86,500	70,900	16.08
1983	89,200	75,200	13.23
1984	97,100	80,700	13.87
1985	99,400	82,100	12.42
1986	116,800	94,100	10.18
1987	128,600	105,000	10.20
1988	141,300	118,000	10.34
1989	140,300	116,000	10.32
1990	149,800	118,700	10.13
1991	148,200	120,000	9.23
1992	137,700	118,000	8.40
1993	143,400	123,900	7.33
1994	144,400	124,400	8.36
1995	154,200	131,000	7.96
1996	168,400	144,200	7.81
1997	175,500	145,900	7.60
1998	179,800	149,900	6.94
1999	189,100	158,200	7.43
2000	202,200	169,000	8.06
2001	209,300	175,000	6.97
2002	217,800	175,600	6.54
2003	248,400	190,200	5.82
2004	279,200	212,400	5.84
2005	275,000	215,000	5.87

Source: U.S. Census Bureau

alarming 16 percent in 1981 and 1982, the median price rose from $69,500 in 1981 to $75,200 in 1983, and the average price rose from $82,600 in 1981 to $89,200 in 1983.

As such, we can't just assume that increasing interest rates automatically causes a price decline or a real estate slump. Other factors come into play for prices to go down, as they did in 1989 and 1992. Typically, price drops are caused by job losses, a recession, and/or war (such as the Gulf War). But even factors like job losses and recessions are often local in nature and scope.

And remember this important point: Real estate statistics are almost always for the single-family homeowner, not the investor. Yes, the interest rate does concern the investor. In fact, the interest rate really affects the investor more than the owner. Few investors will accept much negative cash flow (caused by high interest rates), but many owners will accept a higher mortgage payment because they still have to have a place to live. When it's time to move because of a job transfer or because they want the right school district, most owners aren't going to fuss over a mortgage payment that is a few hundred dollars more.

But the prices you see in Figure 3.2 are for single-family homes. Investors comprise only a very small portion of this market. On the other hand, if we are talking about duplexes, triplexes, quads, and larger apartment complexes, these all relate to real estate investors. These investors don't really care about the prices of houses, except in a general information way. The reason is because the price of multifamily properties, what investors are chasing, can go with the trend of house prices or against them. If home prices are rising, keeping more potential buyers locked out of the market, then more folks have to rent. This forces up rents in that market, which forces up the value of multifamily properties. But then, after some time, as we've seen in the post-boom market, high prices take their toll, buyers back off, and more houses stay on the market, which drives prices down again. This often will cause residential multifamily properties to drop in value as well. The best way to judge what is going on with multifamily properties is not to follow house prices, but to follow the going GRM (gross rent multiplier) or the cap rate (for commercial property), as we've discussed earlier.

For the real estate investor, it comes back to two things: local market conditions and cash flow on a particular property. So how did sellers sell their properties when interest rates were at 16 percent? They financed their own deals. When buyers can't cash flow properties (which is not to say that most of the single-family homes were bought by investors and rented, of course) at current rates with conventional lenders, sellers typically are forced to offer seller financing at more reasonable rates. That's how real estate investors stay in the game during times of high interest rates.

If rates are at 12 percent, buyers will be steering away from most properties because this rate will cause negative cash flow. A seller who needs to sell his or her property might offer seller financing at 7 percent, for example, to close the deal. In our earlier example of a $200,000 loan, that financing adjustment would lower the buyer's mortgage payment from $2,057 (at 12 percent interest) to $1,330. In all likelihood, the conventional mortgage would result in negative cash flow on the property, while the seller financing would result in positive cash flow.

INFLATION

One would think that inflation plays a key part in the appreciation of real estate. As inflation increases, real estate, like other commodities, should rise also, right? And if inflation is quite low, then housing prices should follow suit, right? Not so fast. Take a look at Figure 3.3, which compares mortgage rates, median home prices, and inflation rates over the past 30 years.

Can you see a pattern between mortgage rates and prices, and prices and inflation? Neither can I. There doesn't seem to be any

FIGURE 3.3 *Mortgage Rates, Median Home Prices, and Inflation Rates*

Year	Mortgage Rate	Median Home Price	Inflation Rate (CPI)*
1975	9.04%	$ 38,600	9.1%
1976	8.86	44,600	5.8
1977	8.84	48,600	6.5
1978	9.63	54,800	7.6
1979	11.19	63,800	11.3
1980	13.77	64,000	13.5
1981	16.63	69,500	10.3
1982	16.08	70,900	6.2
1983	13.23	75,200	3.2
1984	13.87	80,700	4.3
1985	12.42	82,100	3.6
1986	10.18	94,100	1.9
1987	10.20	105,000	3.6
1988	10.34	118,000	4.1
1989	10.32	116,000	4.8
1990	10.13	118,700	5.4
1991	9.23	120,000	4.2
1992	8.40	118,000	3.0
1993	7.33	123,900	3.0
1994	8.36	124,400	2.6
1995	7.96	131,000	2.8
1996	7.81	144,200	3.0
1997	7.60	145,900	2.3
1998	6.94	149,900	1.6
1999	7.43	158,200	2.2
2000	8.06	169,000	3.4
2001	6.97	175,000	2.8
2002	6.54	175,600	1.6
2003	5.82	190,200	2.3
2004	5.84	212,400	2.7
2005	5.87	215,000	3.4
2006	6.36	n/a	n/a

* The Consumer Price Index (CPI), commonly referred to as the inflation rate, is a measure of the average change in prices paid by consumers for a fixed market basket of goods and services.

Source: U.S. Department of Labor, Bureau of Labor Statistics

correlation between these figures. When mortgage rates were out of sight, at over 16 percent in 1981 and 1982, home prices should have decreased, right? But they didn't. In 1981, they jumped from $64,000 to $69,500. In 1982, they jumped from $69,500 to $70,900. Go figure.

When mortgage rates came down in 1992 from 9.23 to 8.40 percent, home prices should have increased, right? But they didn't. They went down from $120,000 to $118,000.

Now let's look at the inflation rates. When homes had a lot of help from inflation from 1979 to 1980, at an annual clip of 11.3 percent, what happened? Home prices froze. The bump from $63,800 in 1979 to $64,000 in 1980, or a $200 increase, was negligible. The bump from 1980 to 1981 also didn't match or come close to the inflation rate of 13.5 percent.

Let's now go in the other direction. In 1986, when inflation was at a meager 1.9 percent, home prices jumped from $94,100 to $105,000, or about 11.6 percent. In 1998, with only 1.6 percent inflation, prices jumped from $149,900 to $158,200, or about 5.5 percent. Again in 2002, inflation was only 1.6 percent, yet the median home price jumped from $175,600 to $190,200, or about 8.3 percent. Does this make sense? I didn't think so either.

So what does this tell us? Just that we can't predict where home prices will be based on mortgage rates or inflation rates. You are better off concentrating on real estate fundamentals for your local market, such as:

- Inventory (number of houses, condos, or apartments on the market), which affects supply and demand
- The GRM (gross rent multiplier) for residential multifamily properties, and the cap rate for commercial properties
- Employment rate
- In- or out-migration of residents
- Available land for new developments
- Rent rates

REAL ESTATE CYCLES

Perhaps we should also watch real estate cycles. Have you heard about the decade slump cycle? There's one theory that holds that real estate slumps around the turn of a new decade. But that doesn't hold water with our records (see again, Figure 3.3). Indeed, there was a one-year slump from 1979 to 1980, and a four-year slump from 1988 to 1992, but look at the next decade. Prices moved from $149,900 in 1998 to $158,200 in 1999 to $169,000 in 2000 to $175,000 in 2001. The slump occurred in 2002, when prices only jumped $600 from $175,000 in 2001 to $175,600 in 2002.

There are others, with far more experience than me (at least in commercial real estate), who suggest that real estate runs in cycles. Craig Hall, in *Timing the Real Estate Market,* suggests that these cycles exist and that you should buy at or near the bottom and sell at or near the top. I certainly respect what Mr. Hall has done in his real estate career, but his book contains no charts or figures for these cycles with actual, historical numbers. Certainly, prices in any market do go up and down, but are these "cycles" that follow a pattern? If so, they would repeat themselves and could be predicted. But if we look at the past 30 years of single-family home prices, we don't see such a cycle. Granted, cycles would be harder to quantify for commercial properties, but, if they do exist, they should be reflected in historical numbers.

I would tend to agree with Gerald Marcil, one of the authors of *How to Build a Real Estate Empire,* who states:

I don't know when the market will peak or when it will bottom out. I stay in it at all times and just try to buy the best deals at any given time. My strategy is buy high, low, and in the middle. It will average out over the long haul. I have only seen income property come down twice in 30

years (1981–1982 and 1991–1994). How can I predict five
years out of 30?[1]

Marcil's advice is sound, I think. If you wait and try to time the
market, what will happen if you are wrong? I know people who
thought the real estate market would crash in 2002 or 2003 and
so they didn't buy. They kept waiting for the "bubble" to burst. It
never did, and they lost tens of thousands of dollars in lost opportunity cost. Now, many can't afford to buy because the boom
run was so long and went so far that they were priced out of the
market. If the market did tank, an investor should have been fine
anyway. Why? Because the investor's mortgage payment and rents
didn't change. An investor would still have the same cash flow as
he did before the market tanked, if not much better, due to rehab
and increased rents. The only thing that would have changed is a
number on his net worth statement; that is, the value listed for a
particular property in his assets column would have gone down,
thus decreasing his overall net worth. On paper, anyway.

My advice is, don't try to time the market. Just buy when it
makes sense. Buy when you can cash flow a property, or, if you are
buying for a great location, buy when you know you can handle
a little negative cash flow while you upgrade the property and
increase the rents. Regardless of what the newspapers say, or what
real estate forecasts say, you should know whether a real estate
purchase makes sense by the numbers.

4

DIFFERENT APPROACHES TO INVESTING

How one invests in real estate in different types of markets—boom, bust, or balanced—will depend largely on their approach. Some investors have a very long-term view and simply want to buy and hold. Others want to buy, improve the property, raise the rents, sell, and buy a larger property all within two or three years (the "pyramid" approach). Still others want to time the market, buying when everyone else is selling, and selling when everyone else is buying. All of these approaches work, but you must remember that some approaches allow for, or even require, negative cash flow for a period of time. Let's take a look at each approach and analyze how each type of investor works in each particular market.

BUY AND HOLD

A buy-and-hold investor has a simple approach. Buy whenever you can and never sell. That's it. Buy in a boom, a bust, or a balanced market. Never sell. You may desire to pull equity out from time to time to purchase other properties, but never sell your original property. Dr. David Schumacher, perhaps the best proponent of this plan, appropriately called his book, *Buy and Hold: 7 Steps to a Real Estate Fortune.* This approach has a number of inherent advantages:

- Properties in good locations almost always go up in value, especially over the long term.
- A 20-year approach (or longer) allows you to withstand the ups and downs of real estate markets and avoid selling in a weak market, only to regret it later when the market rebounds.
- You avoid the expensive transaction costs (closing costs and brokers' fees).
- You build up equity (assuming a fully amortized loan) as you hold and eventually will own the property free and clear.
- You avoid the need to buy properties at a discount with a long-term view.

The key element to the buy-and-hold approach is this: It's okay to pay full price for a property, or even overpay for a property, as long as it is in a great location that will appreciate significantly over 20 or more years and you can live with the terms.

There are two negatives to this approach. First, negative cash flow. Buying great properties in excellent locations will almost always require you to have negative cash flow for a while, perhaps up to several years. That's a very long time to fork out money from your pocket. One way to look at it is that it's just a forced savings plan. I like the buy-and-hold plan because you can refinance and pull cash out for other properties. I have been buying in premium locations—hot downtown areas and oceanfront on the hottest beach in Florida (at least for me). I have a small negative cash flow on two properties. It just comes with the territory. I make it up in appreciation. Many investors don't like this approach because they see it as speculation. I would retort that it's only speculation if you don't know your market.

But I don't like negative cash flow either, so I'm always keeping my eyes open for a 1031 exchange deal. A 1031 exchange means that the Internal Revenue Service will allow you to roll your gain from the sale of your first property into a second "like-kind" property (meaning another income property), thus delaying payment of capital gains taxes. So I'm currently looking at maybe using a 1031 exchange to sell one of my properties with negative cash flow for a property that will provide positive cash flow. It's not urgent, of course, because my appreciation has been good. However, I have two incentives to exchange now.

First, the market has cooled and prices have stabilized. Neither my property nor one that I would be buying will change too much in price for 2007 (I've already increased all of the rents on the specific property that I have in mind). If anything, 2007 may be the bottom, or close to the bottom, for prices in this real estate market.

Second, the sell option may work better for me than refinancing. Granted, if I sell I'll be hit with closing costs and a broker's commission. But if I refinance to buy another property, I have two disadvantages:

1. I can't pull out all of my equity because lenders will only allow you to get a loan up to 80 percent of the value of your property, less your outstanding mortgage (although some lenders will take a second mortgage behind that to allow you to go up to a 90 percent combined loan-to-value).
2. If I pull out equity on a property that has just a little negative cash flow, imagine how much negative cash flow I'll have if I pull out $100,000 to buy another property. Any positive cash flow from the new property would be negated by the bloodbath I would be taking each month on the first property.

So, in this case, I think the safer route is to sell the first property and "pyramid" up to a second, larger cash-producing property.

To do this, however, I'll have to buy in another market. You may have the same problem in your market, especially if you live in a large city. In my market (Central Florida), one either has to buy in bad areas or in areas over an hour away to get positive cash flow upon closing. Of course, it's a trade-off. The cash flow will be good in another area but the appreciation will not be as good as in Orlando. But, with a new property, I can overcome this a bit by improving the property, which I cannot do again on the Orlando property that I have now. Naturally, I'll have to use a property manager for a new purchase in another market. I currently use a property management company for my property at the beach and it has been great. But one word of advice on picking managers: get a referral.

There is a possible solution to negative cash flow. I have been negotiating on a quadraplex in the hot area of Orlando and the last offer by the seller, if I accepted it, would result in negative cash flow of about $500 per month. When you have a few properties with this kind of negative cash flow it can add up, especially with unexpected repair bills. However, if the property is a great one, in an *outstanding* location, it *may* be worth it. Obviously, you could just put an additional $6,000 in a savings account to cover this negative cash flow for a year. Another option would be to ask the seller to hold a second mortgage, perhaps with delayed payments, so that the property will provide cash flow (or have very little negative cash flow). On this particular property, however, the seller knows that his property is in a killer location, which gives him some leverage in dictating his terms and price. However, because the market has been down and many investors are sitting on the sidelines, I am playing a waiting game to see if the seller will lower the price after the property sits on the market for six months.

Another thing to keep in mind is what I like to call "windfall cash." This property brings in $3,535 per month in rental income.

If I close on the first of the month, I'll get that rent income (pro-rated if I close later in the month), but I won't have a mortgage payment that month. In addition, I'm currently using a buyer broker (who typically shares the commission with the buyer) so I'd also get 1.25 percent of the purchase price, or $7,062, at closing (because the buyer's agent is allocated 2.5 percent of the commission on this property). That would give me a windfall of $10,597 if I purchase the property. This amount of money would carry my negative cash flow for about 21 months—perhaps long enough to raise rents to a level where the property would provide positive cash flow. And I will have captured a "Boardwalk"-type property (which fans of the game Monopoly can appreciate).

The second negative of the buy-and-hold approach is time. If you are buying premium properties at premium prices, you must hold them for years before they begin to break even. But again, if you plan for this negative cash flow, especially if you have it covered in a fashion as I just explained, it becomes less burdensome.

Commercial Property

If you are looking to invest in commercial real estate, the best book on the market (excluding textbooks), in my opinion, is *How to Build a Real Estate Empire,* compiled by the brokerage firm Marcus, Millichap & Green. The book is a compilation of advice and biographies from four of the firm's biggest real estate clients. Two of those clients, Ben Leeds and Gerald Marcil, use the buy-and-hold approach to investing. Leeds, who owns over 1,600 apartments with a market value of over $160,000,000, says this about his approach:

> I regret everything I have ever sold. Nothing has kept up with the value of real estate. The reasons to sell might include a deteriorating market, the need to diversify out of a particular area, or to take a profit if some insane buyer wants to offer much more than a property might be worth.

With that as a background, why I sold and what I sold made sense at the time, but I still regret selling—it was a means to an end. A better process is to refinance and reinvest the proceeds in other investment property. . . . Any investor considering getting out of the market for whatever reason should consider the environment in mid-2005 as a peak. Nevertheless, I am not selling.[1]

Gerald Marcil, who owns 1,647 units (comprised of 817 apartments and 830 other commercial property units), has a similar approach:

I don't know when the market will peak or when it will bottom out. I stay in it at all times and just try to buy the best deals at any given time. My strategy is buy high, low, and in the middle. It will average out over the long haul. I have only seen income property come down twice in 30 years (1981–1982 and 1991–1994). How can I predict five years out of 30?[2]

Like Leeds, Marcil prefers to refinance and maintain properties rather than sell:

I don't like to sell or trade. I prefer to refinance and use that money. . . . Selling should be a last resort. . . ."[3]

Notice that the buy-and-hold approach works just as well with commercial properties as with residential properties. For those with a shorter time frame, let's now look at the pyramid approach.

PYRAMID

A second approach is to buy and sell approximately every two years, pyramiding to a larger property each time. You buy a property, rehab it, increase the rents (which may take a year if a new tenant has a one-year lease), sell it after two years, and buy a larger property with the proceeds. I am currently thinking about doing this with a triplex I own. The property is in a decent but not excellent location (the excellent locations really had ridiculous prices at the time). When I purchased it, the rents were $675, $675, and $625, or $1,975 total. I rehabbed the $625 unit and increased the rent to $850. I then increased the other units to $750 and $725. My monthly total is now $2,325. I purchased this property for $370,000 at a GRM of 15.6 (the lowest of any downtown properties).

Given the current market, I believe I could sell it for a GRM of 16.5, or for $460,350. After you subtract transaction costs and improvements, the net gain would be about $63,000. Add in the original down payment of $74,000 and I would have $137,000 to put down on a new property. The turnaround time would be 13 to 15 months. Now with $137,000, I could purchase a $675,000 property (assuming 20 percent down), or possibly a $1.37 million property (assuming 10 percent down). Putting only 10 percent down would involve more risk, of course, and would make it slightly harder to have positive cash flow (the difference in the payment is not that dramatic). This is an example of how you could pyramid your investment every two years or so.

The other option is to refinance it at the new appraised value of $460,350. Typically, a lender will allow you to pull out equity up to 80 percent of its appraised value, less your debt. For this property, it would look like this:

New appraised value:	$460,350
80% valuation:	$368,280
Current debt:	−$296,000
Amount I could pull out:	$ 72,280

With this available, tax-free (remember, it's loan money) cash, I could buy a $720,000 property (10 percent down), or a $360,000 property (20 percent down). This approach is kind of a "half pyramid"—you are getting a second property while keeping the first property.

This pyramid method was used by William Nickerson, who started buying his first properties during the Great Depression. Nickerson retired financially independent at age 42, notwithstanding a very average salary working for a telephone company until his retirement. Although now out of print, Nickerson's book, *How I Turned $1,000 into a Million in Real Estate in My Spare Time,* is a classic and is one of my favorite real estate books. It is also the best book on this plan of investing.

There are several disadvantages to this approach, however. First, unless you are keeping the first property and refinancing to get the second one, you incur significant transaction costs by selling every two years or so. You have closing costs for buying and selling, and broker commissions when you sell. In addition, unless you are using a 1031 exchange, you will incur federal income taxes as well. Second, you rarely find a property to buy the day after you sell your prior property. As such, you will have "down time" where your appreciation, cash flow, and tax benefits stop while you look for your next property (under a 1031 exchange[4] you have 180 days to find your next property). Third, you must always be looking for your next property because your turnaround time is only about two years.

TIME THE MARKET

A third approach is to time the market. This investor attempts to buy when others are selling, and to sell when others are buying. This is the "buy straw hats in winter" approach to investing made famous by John D. Rockefeller. The problem, of course, is that correctly timing the market is not easy to do. Many investors who are in real estate as a business (as opposed to most who invest in their spare time) use this approach and still find it difficult to time the market perfectly.

Marcel Arsenault, one of the authors of *How to Build a Real Estate Empire,* uses this approach. Arsenault, who owns various office, retail, industrial, and residential holdings throughout the United States, moves in and out of different types of properties as the market changes:

> An important aspect of real estate investing is to understand how to change investment strategy during market shifts. My investment goals have been modified as the market changed. Initially we purchased only value-added or workout properties with high yield and high internal rates of return. That was my strategy from the mid-1980s until 1993. From 1993 to 2003 . . . we sold 30 percent of our original local portfolio and exchanged it into stable, long-term net-leased properties with nation-wide locations. Now we are selling some stable, net-leased portfolios that we will exchange once again into more high-return, value-added deals.[5]

Perhaps the best book on timing the market is Craig Hall's *Timing the Real Estate Market.* Like the other commercial real estate investors, Hall is in real estate as a business. Over 35 years, he has bought, sold, managed, and developed properties valued at over $5 billion. Not ironically, Hall cites William Nickerson's *How*

I Turned $1,000 into a Million in Real Estate in My Spare Time as one of his early guides.

Hall cites his method as contrarian: "Contrarian buyers buy at low points and as close to the bottom as possible, when everyone else is selling. Like me, they buy when there is blood in the streets."[6] Hall also highlighted one of my favorite messages about real estate investing:

> "Real estate is a cash flow business." There it is—the second greatest lie in real estate. . . . [Y]our expenses and capital expenditures will, over time, eat up most or all of your positive cash flow. . . . [Y]ou likely won't make money on the cash flow of your investment during the time that you own it. The time to make money is when you sell.[7]

Naturally, if you hold a property long enough, as in the buy-and-hold approach, you'll have increased rents enough over the years to have a decent positive cash flow (and eventually pay off the mortgage).

Under this type of approach, you buy when prices are just beginning to move up. But how do you know this? If it were that simple, everyone would do it, right? While it is difficult to do it perfectly, Hall cites five indicators of upward moving prices:

1. Positive direction of the general economy
2. Positive job growth (both nationally and locally)
3. Positive money flows (money flowing into real estate)
4. Stable or falling interest rates
5. A positive prevailing psychology in the marketplace (when people are positive about real estate as a favorable investment and prices seem to be going up)[8]

Once purchased, this view suggests that you hold for one "cycle" (two to ten years where prices hit their lows and highs) and sell near the top. But how do you know that you are at the top or that the momentum is starting to move in the other (downward) direction? Hall gives three warning signals suggesting that the upward price momentum is waning, making it a good time to sell:

1. Prices on competitive properties stop going up or are going down.
2. Sellers are asking substantially more than what buyers are willing to pay.
3. The rental market softens (higher vacancies and/or lower rents).[9]

The disadvantage of this type of approach should be obvious. It is very difficult to consistently identify the top and bottom of markets. As you saw in Chapter 2, some very bright people who track the economy and numerous national statistics have been wrong about the timing of our real estate cool down. How, then, can the layman do it?

In my experience, the investors using this type of approach are institutional investors and large commercial investors. That is, this approach requires investors who are in real estate as a business, not as a pure passive investment. Most individual investors have full-time jobs and don't have the time or staff to constantly watch national and local economic indicators so that they can time the market.

So which type of approach is best—buy and hold, pyramid, or the timing method? For most individual investors, the timing method is inappropriate or inapplicable, as mentioned. This leaves either the buy-and-hold or the pyramid approach. Which is best? It's hard to say. I've done both and they both work. Dr. Schumacher provides a 40-year history of the buy-and-hold approach and William Nickerson provides a 40-year history of the pyramid approach. If you wish to see how the numbers might work for each method over 15 years, using 7 percent appreciation and an initial value of $200,000, with rehab in year one, see Figures 4.1, 4.2, and 4.3. Figures 4.2 and 4.3 illustrate how the "refi and buy" and the "sell and pyramid" methods work far better than simply holding a property without buying more. But before you start counting your millions, please understand that it would be very difficult to consistently buy and sell exactly at the two-year mark shown. I offer these examples not so that you can get your brother-in-law to give you money to invest, but rather to illustrate the advantage of the refi and pyramid strategies. I think you'll be happy with your returns.

FIGURE 4.1 *Buy-and-Hold Strategy at 7 Percent Appreciation and 10 Percent Rehab Added Value (with initial purchase price of $200,000 and 10 percent down)*

Number of Years	Value at 7% Appreciation	Added Value from Rehab	Equity
1	$214,000	$20,000	$ 54,000
2	250,380		70,380
3	267,907		87,907
4	286,660		106,660
5	306,726		126,726
6	328,197		148,197
7	351,171		171,171
8	375,753		195,753
9	402,056		222,056
10	430,200		250,200
11	460,314		280,314
12	492,536		312,536
13	527,014		347,014
14	563,905		383,905
15	603,378		423,378

Source: *Investing in Duplexes, Triplexes & Quads,* by Larry B. Loftis (Kaplan Publishing, 2006)

FIGURE 4.2 *Refi-and-Buy Strategy at 7 Percent Appreciation and 10 Percent Rehab Added Value (with initial purchase price of $200,000 and 10 percent down)*

Number of Years	Value at 7% Appreciation	Added 10% Value from Rehab	Total Equity
1	$214,000	$20,000	$54,000
2	$250,380		$70,380
Refi, pulling out $20K in equity, and buy $200K property			
3	$481907	$20,000	$121,907
4	$537,040		$157,040
Refi, pulling out $69K, and buy $690K in properties			
5	$1,312,933	$69,000	$311,933
6	$1,478,668		$408,668
Refi, pulling out $200K (20% down), and buy $1 million in properties			
7	$2,652,175	$100,000	$682,175
8	$2,944,827		$874,827
Refi, pulling out $570K, and buy $2.85 million in properties			
9	$6,200,465	$285,000	$1,565,465
10	$6,939,447		$2,019,447
Refi, pulling out $1.49 million, and buy $7.45 million in properties			
11	$15,396,708	$745,000	$3,771,708
12	$17,271,627		$4,901,627
Refi, pulling out $3.7 million, and buy $18.5 million in properties			
13	$38,275,641	$1,850,000	$9,255,641
14	$42,934,436		$12,064,436
Refi, pulling out $9.5 million, and buy $47.5 million in properties			
15	$96,764,846	$4,750,000	$23,144,846

Source: *Investing in Duplexes, Triplexes & Quads,* by Larry B. Loftis (Kaplan Publishing, 2006)

FIGURE 4.3 *Sell-and-Pyramid Strategy at 7 Percent Appreciation and 10 Percent Rehab Added Value (with initial purchase price of $200,000 and 10 percent down)*

Number of Years	Value at 7% Appreciation	Added 10% Value from Rehab	Total Equity
1	$214,000	$20,000	$54,000
2	$250,380		$70,380
Sell property #1. Buy $703,800 in properties (10% down)			
3	$753,066	$70,380	$190,026
4	$881,087		$247,667
Sell properties #2. Buy $1.24 million in properties (20% down)			
5	$1,326,800	$124,000	$458,467
6	$1,552,356		$560,023
Sell properties #3. Buy $2.8 million in properties (20% down)			
7	$2,996,000	$280,000	$1,036,023
8	$3,505,320		$1,265,343
Sell properties #4. Buy $6.3 million in properties (20% down)			
9	$6,741,000	$630,000	$2,336,343
10	$7,886,970		$2,852,313
Sell properties #5. Buy $14.26 million in properties (20% down)			
11	$15,258,200	$1,426,000	$5,276,513
12	$17,852,094		$6,444,407
Sell properties #6. Buy $32.2 million in properties (20% down)			
13	$34,454,000	$3,220,000	$11,918,407
14	$40,311,180		$14,555,587
Sell properties #7. Buy $72.77 million in properties (20% down)			
15	$77,827,390	$7,277,794	$26,927,835

Source: *Investing in Duplexes, Triplexes & Quads,* by Larry B. Loftis (Kaplan Publishing, 2006)

5

DIFFERENT
APPROACHES TO
SELECTING PROPERTIES

Just as there are different approaches on how to invest in real estate, so there are different approaches as to how to select properties. These approaches may overlap somewhat with the investing approaches outlined in Chapter 4. How you invest in a boom, bust, or balanced market will be affected by both your overall investing approach and your property selection approach. Basically, there are three priority perspectives on choosing a property:

1. Location/appreciation
2. Price/discount
3. Cash flow

Let's analyze each method, understanding how they relate to your overall plan.

LOCATION/APPRECIATION

For the right property, you can afford to pay top dollar.

—Dr. David Schumacher

This perspective on choosing properties suggests buying the best properties in the best locations that you can. Don't worry so much about price. The price you pay will be irrelevant in 20 years. Plan on negative cash flow. This approach is an appreciation play. You are buying a property for its future benefits, not current benefits. This property could be worth a small fortune in 20 years. This perspective lends itself to the buy-and-hold strategy and is the exact method used by Dr. David Schumacher. I sometimes try to follow this location/appreciation approach as well, unless the price is so high that the negative cash flow is unreasonable.

If you read his book, *Buy and Hold,* you'll recall that Dr. Schumacher had negative cash flow on his early properties for *seven* years. I try to limit that time frame to two years or less. Let me here dispel a real estate seminar myth: If you are buying properties in excellent locations that will appreciate well, you're not going to get $3,000 per month in positive cash flow. If you put little money down, as is often suggested, you'll be paying each month just to own the property. We call that negative cash flow. Even with 20 percent down, the property probably will be priced so that it still will not cash-flow. In most instances, the only way to get positive decent cash flow immediately after closing is to buy "C" class properties. These are generally in blue collar to rough neighborhoods with rough tenants. Don't expect these tenants to pay their rent on time. If they don't, do not send your sister to collect. If you live (or invest) in more rural areas, you may be able to get cash flow with class "B" properties (generally, a blue to white collar property in a decent neighborhood). But again, if you buy in this way, you are subverting the location/appreciation approach because these properties will not appreciate well.

In the last chapter, I gave an example of a quad that I am currently negotiating. It is a great property in the hottest part of Orlando. I've had my eye on this property for over two years. It came on the market over a year ago with a listing price of $775,000. While the GRM for this area supported that price at the time, I just felt it was too much. The negative cash flow would have been considerable, even with 20 percent down. I wanted the property, it is in an awesome location, and it is well built and maintained. But the price just made it illogical for a prudent investor. It was difficult to wait, but I knew that if the numbers didn't work for me, they wouldn't work for other investors either.

After about six or seven months on the market, the property was taken off the market and the multiple listing service (MLS). A few months later, the property was repainted and it looks even better. It was put back on the market at $650,000, which made it more enticing, but was still too high. Just about two weeks ago the price was dropped to $599,000 and got my attention once again. I put in an offer of $530,000 and I've heard from the seller's broker that the lowest they will go is $565,000. It would still have negative cash flow at that price, but not for very long, perhaps 18 months. It may take several months sitting on the MLS before the seller thinks about lowering his bottom price; but that's okay. I have time on my side. The market in my area should stay soft until mid-2007 so I don't think the property is going anywhere. I risk losing it, of course, but not many buyers right now are chasing hard after properties that will have negative cash flow. So, I wait and just watch my market. In a few months my broker may get a call from the seller's broker with a new "bottom" price.

PRICE/DISCOUNT

After a certain amount of dickering, the average seller,
especially if his place has been on the market for several months,
will accept an offer 25 percent under his original asking price,
although he would refuse so low an initial offer.

—William Nickerson

There are buyers who have built considerable real estate fortunes
buying property below construction costs.

—Marcus, Millichap & Green[1]

Some investors focus on the price more than any other factor. That is, they want to get a deal. Indeed, if you can purchase a property at 10 to 25 percent under market value, you walk into considerable equity. Others simply seek to purchase a property at a price under the construction cost (in current dollars).

The upside is obvious. But what about the disadvantages? First, few sellers will sell good properties at substantial discounts to market value. In my experience, I've found that owners of investment properties are savvy investors as well. If they were not, they wouldn't own these types of properties. They are not going to give away the farm because they don't know the value of their property. In most cases, you only can buy properties at substantial discounts when the property is distressed (in need of repair) or the sellers are highly motivated due to extenuating circumstances (e.g., foreclosure, divorce, move to another area, etc.).

Oftentimes you hear in real estate seminars that it is easy to buy properties at significant discounts, say 20 to 40 percent, by finding "motivated" sellers. In most cases, however, the motivated sellers, if you find them, are selling their properties at 10 to 20 percent discounts. Typically, to get a property at a discount of over 20 percent, you'd need to purchase it at a foreclosure (or pre-foreclosure) or tax deed sale.[2] But properties acquired at these auctions typically are not quality multifamily or commercial properties (not to mention the ethical issues involved if you are buying a property through a preforeclosure process).

I don't follow this method of seeking properties because of the scarcity of them, the poorer locations, and the other significant purchasing goals such as location and financing. Don't get me wrong. I try to get properties under market value, and if I can find a property for 70 cents on the dollar that can be improved with reasonable costs, I'll do so. But in keeping my eyes open for such deals I'll not overlook a property in an outstanding location that I can get for 90 cents on the dollar with excellent financing.

CASH FLOW

Even as a small-property buyer you should expect the income
to pay off expenses and the mortgage and to net a return
of no less than 6 percent on your personal investment.
—William Nickerson

Many investors will not buy a property that does not have a positive cash flow. That is, there must be something left over from rental income after paying the mortgage payment, taxes, insurance, repairs, and maintenance. Certainly, this is the safest route and every investor would love to have properties that throw off nice cash flow each month. So this is a good and worthy goal for each property you purchase.

The problem, of course, is that few properties that will appreciate well will give you positive cash flow from the date of purchase. I am disappointed at the number of books and seminars touting things like "replace your current income with cash flow from properties," or "make $5,000 to $10,000 per month in cash flow." Of course, those claims sell books and expensive seminars. I know of one seminar speaker (who I don't think owned *any* investment properties) who would tell his audiences that he made $100,000 *per month* in cash flow from his real estate. When I heard that I didn't know whether to laugh or cry. Making that kind of money in net cash flow is just not practicable.

Recall what Craig Hall (see Chapter 4) says: " [Y]ou likely won't make money on the cash flow of your investment during the time that you own it. The time to make money is when you sell."[3] Let's take a look at real numbers to see why it is highly unlikely for you to have significant positive cash flow (where you could replace your current income) from a property (or properties) soon after purchase.

Recall the quad that I am currently negotiating? The asking price has been lowered to $599,000 and I have a counteroffer from the owner at $565,000. This was the second counteroffer and the owner claims it is the last (which may or may not be true; that will probably depend on how long it sits on the market). But let's say that I get the seller down to $560,000. While that may still seem to be expensive for four units, it is lower, at a GRM of 13.2, than the going rate of other multifamily units in the area (with GRMs of 14 to 20). Here's the formula again:

$$\text{GRM} = \text{Purchase price} \div \text{Gross annual rents}$$
$$\$560,000 \div \$42,420 = 13.2$$

The monthly rents are $3,535, or $42,420 per year. The expenses for taxes, insurance, pest control, lawn care, and maintenance are $800 per month. Assume that I put 20 percent down, or $112,000, leaving a mortgage of $448,000. If I finance this property for 30 years (remember that a quad still qualifies as a residential property) at 7.5 percent interest, my monthly mortgage payment is $3,132. Adding in my other monthly expenses of $800 leaves a monthly overhead nut of $3,932. So it looks like this:

Monthly income	$3,535
Monthly expenses	– $3,932
Negative monthly cash flow	($ 397)

Now understand that we are getting the property below market value based on the GRM and comparable sales, we are putting down 20 percent of the purchase price, or $112,000, and we *still* will have negative cash flow of about $400 per month. Now let's say that we were able to get the seller to drop his asking price by *$100,000* (from his listed price of $599,000). If we use a purchase price of $500,000 and put down $100,000, we'd have a mortgage payment of $2,797. Add in our $800 expenses and we'd have an overhead nut of $3,597. Adding in our income of $3,535, we are still in the hole $62 per month.

Let's pretend that we could buy this property at $450,000 (which we could not), or at 75 percent of the asking price, which is 58 percent of the original asking price of $775,000. Putting down $90,000 and financing the balance of $360,000 at the same terms leaves a monthly payment of $2,517. Adding in our $800 expenses leaves us a total overhead nut of $3,317. Subtracting this from our $3,535 income leaves us with a whopping cash flow of $218 per month. So we've put down $90,000 to make $218 per month. And this is a real property with real numbers.

How many properties will you have to own at this pace to replace your income? Recall that we put down $90,000 and had a ridiculously low purchase price of $450,000 rather than a realistic price of $560,000. And just in case you think the $560,000 price is overly high, the GRM notwithstanding, please note that I own another quad less than three blocks away that just appraised for $800,000—and it brings in *less* per month than the quad we are looking at for $560,000.

How are we doing on "replacing our income with cash flow from properties"? Getting close to the $5,000 per month that the books and seminars tout? Recall the words of Craig Hall: "'Real estate is a cash flow business' . . . the second greatest lie in real estate." You don't make money in real estate from cash flow (at least in the early years). You make money when you sell, or refinance.

Naturally, if you are using the buy-and-hold approach and you are buying in good locations, you'll begin to see some nice positive cash flow five to ten years out—perhaps in less time if you are very good in your acquisition, negotiating, and financing skills. Or, you could get it faster by buying in areas that will not appreciate very well. But again, that's a different philosophy. Just remember that, in most cases, you can have nice appreciation or nice cash flow, but not both (at least in the early years of ownership).

HOW TO CHOOSE

So which method will work best for a boom, bust, or balanced market? If you are in a boom market, your property will appreciate quickly. The better the location, the better the appreciation. So, in that market, the location/quality method will provide the most money for you. Assume, for example, that we have a boom market and that you could choose from two properties listed for $600,000:

1. A quad in a terrific location
2. An eight-unit building in a fair location

Assume the following factors:

- Quad—negative cash flow of $500 per month, great tenants, no major repair issues, 14 percent annual appreciation, close proximity to you
- Eight-unit—positive cash flow of $250 per month, a few tenant problems and vacancies, a few repair issues, 8 percent annual appreciation, one hour away from you

If we follow the buy-and-hold strategy, the property in the better location will be our choice for the long term. If we want to pyramid, let's assume that we sell in two years. The numbers might look like this:

Quad—Negative cash flow	($ 12,000)
Appreciation	$168,000
NET GAIN	$156,000
Eight-unit—Positive cash flow	$ 6,000
Appreciation	$ 96,000
NET GAIN	$102,000

The numbers work better for the great location quad. In addition, the quality of life issues (i.e., tenant problems, drive time, repairs) favor the quad as well. Obviously, I've made a number of assumptions to illustrate a comparison, but in my experience, the overall picture would look something like this illustration.

Now what about a bust market? If you are investing for the long term in a buy-and-hold strategy, you really don't care about the market. The fact that your appreciation will be small for a few years doesn't bother you. But if you are buying to pyramid or time the market, you certainly want to buy at a discount and get positive cash flow as well. The good news is, if there is a real estate bust, or even a slump, the prices will be falling anyway. If you also can buy at a discount to the market, that's even better. When prices rebound, your gain will be excellent. Those trying to time the market will be buying as much as possible in a bust, holding for one cycle, and selling near the top when prices rebound.

In a balanced market, most investors will stick to their game plan. Some will focus on the location. Others will try to buy at bargain prices. Still others will just look for cash flow deals. I would just add one more criterion for all buyers: consider deals that might fall just outside of your parameters if you can get excellent financing. Because I have excellent credit and acceptable debt/ equity ratios on my properties, I have a lender that will finance my next quad deal on these terms: 100 percent financing, 8 percent interest, 30-year amortization with no balloon. While I'm looking at a quad, which is residential, it would be an investment property (i.e., I would not live in it). Typically, lenders will only go up to 80 percent on their loan-to-value ratio (LTV), or 90 percent on a combined loan-to-value ratio (CLTV) where two lenders are used. To get 100 percent financing from a single lender on a non-owner-occupied property is very rare. While the financing is attractive, the debt load would increase the negative cash flow, which is present with 20 percent down, to unacceptable levels. But who knows; if I can get the seller down on price, and can close on the first or second of the month, I just might consider it.

At the end of the day, regardless of which method you use for selecting property and your overall approach, you have to be able to live with the terms. If you are shooting for appreciation as your highest priority, you better look closely at your negative cash flow to make sure you can carry it for an extended period of time. In addition, set aside reserves for unexpected repairs or capital improvements. You'll be glad you did.

6

WHAT TYPE OF PROPERTY AND WHICH LOCATIONS ARE SAFEST AGAINST A BUST?

If you are concerned about a real estate market crash, correction, or even slump, you should be paying careful attention to what type or types of real estate will give you the most protection against such a downturn. Your real estate investing options include:

- Raw land (residential, commercial, or agricultural)
- Single-family homes (including condos and town homes)
- Residential multifamily (duplexes, triplexes, and quads)
- Commercial properties (residential multifamily of five units and up, office, retail, strip mall, shopping center, warehouse, industrial)

RAW LAND

There are a number of disadvantages to investing in raw land. First, you can't easily improve it. Indeed, you can make a lot of money if you are able and willing to procure entitlements (e.g., zoning changes, permits, etc.) and can flip it to a developer. However, it takes considerable dollars for engineering fees to lay out a subdivision, office park, or other commercial use; legal fees to secure zoning and permit approvals; and so on. Indeed, some developers make considerable money putting in streets, lights, sewer, and water and selling it to another developer who will complete the project. But this type of investing takes considerable time, skill, and money. It's a high-risk, high-reward game. As such, it's not for most people who invest in real estate on a part-time basis.

Second, unless you get a zoning change or buy it just as a new road or highway exit is announced, raw land appreciates very slowly. You can't force appreciation quickly by doing cosmetic improvements or getting more tenants. Some real estate companies buy large tracts of land just to hold them for long-term appreciation, often for 10 to 20 years. In most instances they will pay cash for the property. For the average investor, this is not an option. Most investors would need to carry a mortgage on the property, which reveals another disadvantage: no cash flow. Yes, if the property was zoned agricultural you could let a farmer or rancher put some cows or horses on it for a minimal fee, but that's not likely to cover your overhead nut of mortgage and taxes. Don't get me wrong, it does happen, and if you come across a deal where you can hold land on the outskirts of town and cover your overhead nut with agricultural use, by all means, consider it.

Third, because the lender has more risk with raw land, investors will typically only be able to finance 50 to 60 percent of the purchase price with a conventional lender. With 40 to 50 percent down, the investor's yield or return on investment is greatly diminished. In fact, most investors in raw land purchase the properties outright (i.e., no mortgage).

Finally, if the market experiences a severe economic, construction, or development downturn, raw land probably will have few buyers. And the buyers that may be around will be "vulture" buyers looking to steal a property. If you are in a situation in which you really must sell the property, the raw land investor might be required to sell at a great discount to his or her purchase price. On the other hand, if *you* are the vulture buyer with plenty of cash, you could snap up quality acres of land at bargain prices. In fact, this is what many investors are waiting for with the current post-boom market. Some are expecting nice discounts, while others are hoping for a real estate crash thinking that they can steal properties.

SINGLE-FAMILY HOMES

Single-family homes are a good, but perhaps not the safest, investment for real estate investors during times of downturn or crash. Never buy a house to later flip it without improving the property. Many investors purchased condos in Miami during the 2005 condo craze without any intention of improving the property. They simply figured the frenzy would always continue. Many now are stuck holding those condos and cannot sell them without reducing the price and taking a loss. And don't confuse buying a home to live in with a real estate investment, per se. Granted, you may see your home as an investment, particularly during a boom period. However, as Robert Kiyosaki mentioned in *Rich Dad, Poor Dad,* your house is generally a liability, not an investment. That is, it costs you money; it doesn't make you money. You not only have a mortgage payment, you have taxes, insurance, maintenance, pest control, and lawn care expenses. In many cases, you can also add homeowner association fees. This generally amounts to a significant overhead nut each month that no one else (e.g., tenants) pays for. But if you are living in it, you get the benefit of shelter, a nice family environment, and so on.

If you rent out a single-family home, it is indeed an investment, but you have a number of disadvantages. First, most single-family homes won't provide cash flow. For example, your overhead nut might be $2,000 a month but you can only rent it out for $1,500. It's difficult because you have only one revenue source. Compare that with a quad, which might have about the same mortgage payment and overhead, but may draw two or three times as much in income because you have four renters. In our scenario above, few quads will charge less than $500 per unit, per month, in rent. It's all relative to your area and the quality of the property, of course. In my area, I just rented out a small one-bedroom apartment for $725 per month in one property, and another small one-bedroom apartment for $850 in another property. If you live in a small town, however, the going rate might be $450 per month, but the overall cost of the property will be commensurately low as well.

Which brings us to the next disadvantage of a house: the vacancy risk. If you own a rental house and have one vacancy, what is your overall vacancy rate? One hundred percent, right? And who covers the mortgage, taxes, insurance, and maintenance during that vacancy? You do. Now if that property was a quad, on the other hand, and you had a vacancy, the overall vacancy rate would be only 25 percent. As such, the rent from your other three tenants would likely still cover your overhead nut (or come close). So, without considering what the market is doing, residential multifamily is generally safer than a single-family home.

The advantage of investing in single-family homes is that there is a plethora of information on historical prices and forecasts. If you can generally determine the inherent value of a house and predict the price trend for your market, you stand to make considerable money. Fortunately, most of the research data is in this area. Almost all of the boom or bust statistics are looking at single-family homes, rather than multiunit properties or even commercial properties. Recall again our chart from Chapter 1 on recent real estate crashes. Notice in Figure 6.1 the severe impact that a crash would have on a buyer who bought at the wrong time (the beginning) of a downturn.

FIGURE 6.1 *Recent Real Estate Busts (Measured from Market Top to Bottom)*

City	Average Price Drop	Years	Years to Recover
Oklahoma City	−26.0%	1983–88	15
Austin	−25.8	1986–90	8
Houston	−22.0	1986–90	15
Los Angeles	−20.7	1990–96	10
Honolulu	−16.0	1994–99	9
Peoria	−15.4	1981–85	8
Detroit	−12.2	1981–84	6

Source: Local Market Monitor, CNNmoney.com

If you had purchased a home in Oklahoma City, for example, as a primary residence, that's one thing. You could just stay in the house and wait it out. Your mortgage payment didn't change. Also, you bought that house because you liked the area or the schools or whatever. But if you bought it as an investment, you bought it to make money on it, either through appreciation or cash flow, or both. If you bought for appreciation, you are hosed. If you bought for cash flow, you might have still been okay, but you certainly could not expect to sell and trade up for many years. Now if you had this information and bought in 1988 or 1989, near the tail end of that real estate down cycle, you'd have made a terrific investment.

Most investors in single-family homes are buying them for appreciation, not cash flow (since there will rarely be much cash flow in the first place). In general, single-family homes will, in an up market, appreciate faster than multifamily housing. However, remember that you can force appreciation through improving the property. If an investor improves a property through rehab, that obviously lessens the risk in a market crash. If the investor buys the property at a discount *and* improves the property, that should eliminate the risk.

The other risk with single-family homes as an investment property is initial vacancy. Very few homes are sold with a renter in them. Almost always, the property will be vacant upon closing. As such, regardless of whether you are rehabbing the property (which increases the amount of time you have a hole in your pocket), you will have at least a month or two of major negative cash flow while you try to rent it out or improve it and rent it out. With a multifamily property, you walk into cash flow unless you buy a building with a 100 percent vacancy. If you do that, don't tell anyone you read my books!

Finally, a crash is usually caused by major job losses in a certain market. If that happens, those losing jobs generally will seek the cheapest housing. What is cheaper to rent, a house or a small apartment? Obviously, an apartment. As a result, landlords of single-family homes will have the most vacancies. Therefore, apartments are the safest properties to own during a downturn.

Bubble-Proof Markets

If you prefer to invest in single-family homes, you certainly want to know which markets are expected to go up, down, or otherwise are considered safe. On October 25, 2006, *Business 2.0* announced its top five bubble-proof housing markets. As I mentioned earlier, real estate statistics are almost always for single-family homes. According to *Business 2.0,* then, these are the safest cities in which to own homes:

1. Boston
2. San Francisco
3. New York
4. Los Angeles
5. Seattle

Typically, as big-city incomes rise, home prices follow suit. In addition, these cities all have diverse economies. They are less susceptible to a single industry downturn than other big cities (e.g., Detroit and the automobile industry, Houston and Dallas and the oil and gas industry, etc.). Here are the specific reasons why *Business 2.0* likes these five cities.

Boston

Median home price: $421,000
Population: 575,000

With the greatest number of colleges and universities in the country, Boston garners the top bubble-proof spot due to its intellectual character. Boston also boasts other world-class cultural institutions, such as the Boston Fine Arts Museum and the Boston Ballet, as well as a great historical tradition, seen in its architecture and neighborhoods. It's also home to a thriving mutual fund industry, which has boosted the city's share of high-income earners. While Boston has weathered an overheated real estate market in recent years—and prices could yet drop in the short run—it is poised well for the long term.

San Francisco

Median home price: $776,000
Population: 735,000

San Francisco's steep hills and glorious views keep real estate in high demand in the city. In addition, the city's diverse economy insulates it from an economic downturn due to one industry's decline. The city's strong public and private universities and vibrant computer industries in nearby Silicon Valley add to its strength.

New York

Median home price: $504,000
Population: 8.1 million

New York is the financial, investment banking, advertising, and media capital of the world. It may be the creative arts capital of the world as well. From Madison Avenue to Broadway to Wall Street, Carnegie Hall to Times Square, New York will always be a thriving business and cultural center. Much of that business activity is generated from New York's capital markets, which in turn creates many well-heeled industry professionals. In addition, land is extremely limited in New York.

Additional information. Brown Harris Stevens (BHS), a large real estate firm in New York, released in October 2006 its New York City *Residential Market Report* for the third quarter of 2006. In this report, BHS's chief economist, Gregory Heym, predicted strong demand and steady prices for the Manhattan market. The report also seemed to indicate that Manhattan really didn't have much of a slowdown from the third quarter of 2005 to the third quarter of 2006. While the city's average apartment price of $1.1 million was 4 percent lower from the third quarter in 2005, the average size of apartments sold was 3 percent smaller from the year before. Likewise, the average condo sale of $1.2 million was down 6 percent from the year before, but the average condo size was also down 5 percent.[1]

Los Angeles

Median home price: $472,000
Population: 3.9 million

Los Angeles is the entertainment capital of the world, and produces most of the country's movies, television shows, and commercials. This factor ensures a constant stream of newcomers seeking fame and fortune. In addition, the glamour and glitz of L.A., from Rodeo Drive to Beverly Hills to the Oscars, from the Lakers to the beaches, always will attract the affluent. But the city also has more mundane industries, such as aerospace, electronics, and sports clothes manufacturing, that make the economy diverse and strong.

Seattle

Median home price: $339,000
Population: 563,000

Seattle is both a beautiful city and a strong commercial center. It is well known as the epicenter of the software industry, thanks to Bill Gates and Microsoft. But it is also the headquarters for Amazon.com and Starbucks. As such, it has a strong employment base.

Additional information. In the period from September 2005 to September 2006, while most home markets decreased in value, median Seattle home prices increased 4.4 percent. However, Seattle's September home price dropped from July and August 2006. Sales also dropped 16 percent from the year before, and the number of properties in inventory was up 30 percent. The fact that Seattle prices actually increased for the 12 months from 2005 to 2006 shows the city's housing stability. The director of the Washington Center for Real Estate Research has forecast that the city's median home prices will match the rate of inflation, or 3 percent.[2]

If you live in or by one of these cities, or have a relative in one of these cities, perhaps one of these cities might be a place to park some of your investment dollars. In Chapter 10, I'll give you the latest reports on the most undervalued and overvalued markets across the country. You'll definitely see buying opportunities near you.

RESIDENTIAL MULTIFAMILY PROPERTIES

According to the National Council of Real Estate Investment Fiduciaries (NCREIF), multifamily property investment returns exceeded all other property returns by 63 basis points in a study measuring a ten-year period from 1995 to 2004. Additionally, the NCREIF concluded that investing in multifamily properties is less risky, showing a volatility of just over one-half of a composite of all property types over that period.[3] As you might have guessed, the NCREIF conducts research on behalf of institutional investors like insurance companies that invest millions of dollars each year in large apartment and other commercial properties. Almost all of its research and reasoning as to why multifamily properties are safer than other types of properties applies to the small investor investing in 2- to 20-unit properties.

I've already addressed the general issue of safety at length in my earlier book, *Investing in Duplexes, Triplexes & Quads: The Fastest and Safest Way to Real Estate Wealth*. In this chapter, however, I'll highlight the general safety features of multifamily properties, and also address, in particular, safety against a real estate bust or major downturn. I firmly believe that residential multifamily properties are by far your safest investment. Here's why.

General Real Estate Safety of Multifamily Properties

1. **Risk of vacancy.** If you have a house for rent and you have a vacancy, what is your overall vacancy rate? One hundred percent, right? If you own a quad and you have a vacancy, what is your overall vacancy rate? Twenty-five percent. If your rental house is vacant (I know from personal experience!), what are your expenses? Mortgage payment, property taxes, insurance, utilities, pest control, and yard maintenance. Who pays that while the property is vacant? You do. And if you don't get a renter soon, *you* will become a motivated seller! When your quad has a vacancy, on the other

hand, the other renters will still cover most or all of your expenses. You have substantially less financial risk.

2. Economies of scale. If you own four houses, you probably will not have them all on the same street. As such, it becomes more of a chore to manage them. You will have to go to different locations to show them and repair them, and you may well have different service people to work on them. For example, your lawn care person may not be willing or able to go to four different places to mow. With a quad, however, you collect four rent payments, but you have only one yard maintenance bill. The same is true for insurance and property taxes. It just becomes easier to achieve cash flow with multiple units in one property.

3. Less competition. When you are looking to buy a single-family home, you generally compete with three potential groups: prospective homeowners, flippers who want to resell it, and buy-and-hold investors who want to rent it. With a multifamily property, your competition generally only includes the latter.

4. Better rent-to-cost ratio. If you buy a multifamily property, your rent-to-cost ratio is better. For example, if you bought a house for $250,000, you might not be able to rent it for more than $1,300 per month. Assume that you put down 10 percent so that your mortgage loan amount is $225,000. At today's rate of about 6.5 percent interest, amortized over 30 years, your mortgage payment would be $1,422 per month. Now let's add property taxes of about $312 per month, insurance of about $104 per month, and pest control and yard maintenance of about $130 per month, and you're at a total overhead nut of $1,968 per month. You now have negative cash flow of $668 per month. Now let's assume that the $250,000 property was a triplex with monthly rent of $700 per unit. Assuming the same expenses, you now have a positive cash flow of $132 per month, or a positive swing of $800. Obviously, these numbers will vary by market. Suffice it to say, however, that it's easier to reach positive cash flow when you have multiple units.

5. Post-closing benefits. A multifamily property has a tremendous advantage over a house immediately after closing. When you buy a house, it's almost always vacant at closing. Very few houses will be sold with a tenant residing in it. If the prior owner is using it as a personal residence, that owner moves out. In most cases, the house will be vacant when you get it, so you move into zero cash flow and immediate stress to find a tenant quickly. If you don't find a tenant immediately, there's that big overhead nut that you'll be covering.

With a multifamily property, it's just the opposite. Almost always, the property will be partially or completely occupied. Smart landlords make sure the property is fully occupied when they sell so that they can get a higher asking price. This adds to your safety in two ways. First, your overhead nut is covered from day one—you walk into cash flow. Second, you should walk away from the closing table with money.

In our prior example of the triplex, we had three renters paying $700 each, or $2,100 total. If we close on the first of the month, we get all of those rents, plus the security deposits. In most cases, the deposits equal one month's rent. As such, we'd leave the closing table with $4,200 (or apply it to closing costs). If we close later in the month, the rents are simply prorated. Because we won't have a mortgage payment the first month, and taxes and insurance will usually be escrowed at closing, we really have a nice windfall. So, at the single-family house closing, you walk away with zero at closing and have to scramble to find a tenant, while the multifamily property gives you $4,200 (or whatever the prorated amount is) at closing and you walk into cash flow with all of your expenses covered.

6. Easiest to improve. With a house purchase, you cannot rent the house or get any cash flow until you have rehabbed it (which you want to do to add value). Again, you are walking into negative cash flow. And how long will it take to rehab it? One month? Two? Three? I have some friends who bought a condo to rehab and flip, but, because they did the work themselves whenever they could get to it, it took them over six months before they could put it on the market. And that's not selling it; that's just putting it on the market. Do the math on that. Negative cash flow plus carrying costs plus opportunity cost equals a disaster. What's worse, it is still unsold after being on the market for five months. They will soon have sat on a vacant condo for a year with no income. Yes, that sucking sound is from the siphon running from their bank accounts to that property. Don't try this at home.

The beauty of multiple units is that you can rehab them one at a time. When I bought the quad that I now live in, it was fully occupied at closing. One month later the tenant in the nicest unit moved out as her lease expired. I moved into that unit, declared homestead as a personal residence to decrease my tax bill, and began rehabbing that unit. About the time I was mostly finished, a second unit vacated per its lease terms. I then rehabbed that unit. Then came unit 3 and then 4. At no time did I have two units vacant at the same time. I always have had three tenants paying the bills while I updated open units. That's safety.

7. Benefits of personal residence. A residential multifamily property (i.e., two to four units) will give you two benefits that no other type of property can give you. First, if you will live in it, you can basically live *rent free* (or very close thereto). If you have a quad and live in one of the units, the rent from the other three units should cover your overhead nut. Second, since you are living in one of the units as a personal residence, you can declare a home-stead on it and reduce your property taxes. The same goes for selling it. Because it is, in fact, a personal residence, you can sell it and pocket all of the gain tax free (up to $250,000 for singles, $500,000 for married couples) if you live in it at least two years.

Safety Against a Bust or Real Estate Downturn

Let's assume the worst—a real estate meltdown. Your market has severe job losses. Many cannot make their mortgage payments and lose their properties to foreclosure. Sellers can't sell their homes. The market is saturated with houses for sale. Prices drop. What do most people do at this point? Look for more expensive housing? Of course not. They will be looking for cheaper housing. And what's the cheapest housing—a house, condo, town home, or apartment? Generally, the apartment will be the cheapest housing. If it gets really bad, many will look for a small one-bedroom, one-bath apartment. You don't find many houses of that size. So more renters will be chasing apartments than houses. Which brings us to our next benefit for multifamily properties if there is a major downturn in the real estate market.

If more people are chasing apartments, what does that do to the apartment rents in that area? They go up, naturally, as a result of supply and demand. So, while the real estate market could be tanking, and house prices could be drastically falling, rents could be going up. Not only does that improve cash flow for the multi-family property owner, it also increases his or her net worth.

Recall again how residential multifamily properties are valued: by the GRM, gross rent multiplier. Just take the purchase price and divide it by the gross rents for the year to determine the GRM. If the going rate of the GRM in your area is 13, for example, and your overall rents increase by $200 per month, you've increased your property's value by $31,200 ($200 × 12 months × 13) in the blink of an eye. So, it's very possible to have multifamily properties increasing in value while the surrounding single-family homes are decreasing in value.

For all of these reasons, residential multifamily properties are the safest real estate investments, regardless of the market. Having said that, you can still take advantage of buying single-family homes as those opportunities arise. The other general guidelines always apply: work to get the best locations, good financing, and reasonable purchase prices (and discounts where you can). Take what the market gives you.

COMMERCIAL PROPERTIES

Commercial properties include multifamily dwellings of five or more units, office buildings, retail plazas, strip malls, shopping centers, warehouses, and industrial buildings. Few individual investors play in this market as the cost of these properties is typically cost prohibitive. In addition, the time requirements for research and infrastructure development (not to mention dealing with city hall) are enormous. The stakes are generally much higher here than with homes or small apartment buildings. As such, most of the players in this category of real estate are real estate companies.

You may also know that these types of properties are highly vulnerable to real estate busts. Did you hear about the "see-through" office buildings in Houston in the early 1980s? *See-through buildings* is developer jargon for empty spec office buildings, graveyard skeletons of failed speculative real estate gambles. Many big office buildings in Houston during this time were so empty that one could literally see through them. For the average individual investor, I'd just caution you to stay with the safest types of real estate during weak or bust markets: residential housing. While people may lose jobs in a bad economy and businesses may close their doors, people still need a roof over their heads. Unless you are in real estate as a business (meaning you don't have another day job), stick to residential properties. This category of real estate investing requires less skill, less money, less time, and, most importantly in a downturn, less risk.

Chapter

7

HOW TO INVEST IN
EACH TYPE OF MARKET

In the last chapter, we saw briefly how to select a property in each type of market. In Chapter 4, we saw how to invest using three different approaches. Now let's put it all together, using an overall investing approach with a property selection approach and applying these guidelines in different markets.

First, however, remember that good investors make money in all real estate markets. Sometimes, they make their money in different ways. I often hear complaints about why someone can't buy real estate. For example, a common objection is that in a boom market the prices are too high and it's impossible to cash-flow the property. Similarly, an objection for a bust market is that the prices are good but the interest rates are high and appreciation is low. But do you realize that real estate is bought and sold every day in every type of market? If the numbers don't work for you, how are the other guys doing it?

THE EQUALIZING EFFECT

We saw in Chapter 3 that for single-family homes, prices and interest rates don't always exactly coincide. With investment real estate, however, markets often have an equalizing effect. When interest rates are very low, prices go up because buyers can afford to pay a higher mortgage payment and still cash-flow their property. When interest rates are high, prices come down because mortgage payments increase and owners don't want properties that have negative cash flow. There is often an equalizing effect with each scenario, which results in a mortgage payment that comes out about the same.

Let's take a look at this equalizing effect by going back and looking at the quad that I am currently negotiating to purchase. In early 2005, a raging boom market, the property was listed for $775,000. It's a beautiful quad in an outstanding location, but it didn't sell. My guess is that it would have sold for $675,000 if marketed near that price. Interest rates at the time were about 6.25 percent. If I purchased that property on those terms, my mortgage payment on a 30-year mortgage, with 20 percent down, would have been $3,325. Now let's move to the more balanced market of late 2006. The property is currently listed for $599,000, but I have a counteroffer from the seller stating that I can purchase it at $565,000. While that is a little higher than I am currently willing to pay, let's run the numbers. Interest rates for a non-owner-occupied quad will run about 7.75 percent. If I purchased it on those terms, also with 20 percent down, my mortgage payment would be $3,238. Notice that the difference in purchase price is $110,000, but the monthly payment amount only differs by $87. Do you see the equalizing effect?

Now assume that we hit a bust market in 2008. Interest rates have jumped, let's say, to 11 percent. Can you estimate where the prices would be? For this property, I'd expect a GRM in the neighborhood of 10. That would put our purchase price at $424,000 (monthly rents of $3,535 × 12 = $42,420 × 10 = $424,200). Our mortgage payment would be $3,230. See the equalizing effect? Let's review the numbers:

Market	Sales Price	Loan	Interest Rate	Mortgage Payment
Boom	$675,000	$540,000	6.25	$3,325
Balanced	$565,000	$452,000	7.75	$3,238
Bust	$424,000	$339,200	11	$3,230

Understand that sellers want to get top dollar for their properties and buyers want to keep their mortgage payments in line with rents so that they have positive cash flow (or as little negative cash flow as possible). There is always ongoing tension. The sellers want the same prices that occurred in the latest good market, even though the market has changed. The buyers don't want to pay the last market prices because they know the market has changed and interest rates have climbed. Oftentimes, it's a standoff to see who will flinch first.

In my Orlando market, this is happening as I write. The market has moved from boom to balanced. However, sellers still want the boom prices. But buyers have been refusing to pay those prices knowing the market has cooled. For the past six months, most real estate investors have been sitting on the sidelines waiting for prices to drop. I'm one of them. Sellers have been refusing to lower prices much. It's the ultimate poker game. As with most things, there will be some adjustment from both sides. Sellers are waiting longer now to sell or are reducing prices just a bit (5 to 10 percent). For the first time in six months, the inventory of homes on the market decreased this past month. The slump appears to be almost over.

Figure 7.1 will illustrate generally what happens in each market to cause this equalization.

FIGURE 7.1 *Market Equalization*

Market Type	Interest Rates	Cash Flow	Price	Appreciation
Balanced	Medium	Medium	Medium	Medium
Boom	Low	Low	High	High
Bust	High	High	Low	Low

Let's look at the rents of the quad I'm considering now and apply different market scenarios. The rents for this property are $3,535 per month. This is a great property in a hot area so the price will be high (as will appreciation). Let's estimate the numbers in a boom, balanced, and bust market.

Boom Market

Here's how the numbers would have looked had the seller sold the property in the 2005 boom market:

Price	$675,000
GRM	15.9
Interest rate	6.25%
Down payment	20% ($135,000)
Mortgage payment	$3,325
Other expenses	$ 800 (taxes, insurance, pest control, yard maintenance)
Mortgage and expenses	$4,125
Rental income	$3,535
Negative cash flow	($ 590) (not including deductions and depreciation)
Appreciation	10–20% ($67,500–$135,000)

Balanced Market

Here's what the numbers might look like in a more balanced market (using late 2006 as an example):

Price	$565,000
GRM	13.3
Interest rate	7.75%
Down payment	20% ($113,000)
Mortgage payment	$3,238
Other expenses	$ 800 (taxes, insurance, pest control, yard maintenance)
Mortgage and expenses	$4,038
Rental income	$3,535
Negative cash flow	($ 503) (not including deductions and depreciation)
Appreciation	6–10% ($33,900–$56,500)

If we were to run the numbers again using a GRM of 11, which would also be within the balanced market parameters (but probably not for the location of this property), we'd basically break even each month.

Price	$467,000
GRM	11
Interest rate	7.75%
Down payment	20% ($93,400)
Mortgage payment	$2,677
Other expenses	$ 800 (taxes, insurance, pest control, yard maintenance)

Mortgage and expenses	$3,477
Rental income	$3,535
Negative cash flow	($ 58) (not including deductions and depreciation)
Appreciation	6–10% ($28,020–$46,700)

Bust Market

Now let's run the numbers for a hypothetical bust market:

Price	$297,000
GRM	7 (the GRM could be lower if more units or worse location)
Interest rate	11%
Down payment	20% ($59,400)
Mortgage payment	$2,263
Other expenses	$ 800 (taxes, insurance, pest control, yard maintenance)
Mortgage and expenses	$3,063
Rental income	$3,535
Positive cash flow	$ 472 (not including deductions and depreciation)
Appreciation	0–5% ($0–$14,850, but could be negative if not a great location)

As you can see, we don't realize a significant positive cash flow for a great property in a hot location until we encounter a bust market. In most other markets, we have negative cash flow or break even. That's why most buy-and-hold buyers who want great locations plan on negative cash flow for several years. Note, of course, that there are many factors that would affect our numbers. The following five items should be considered in your calculations of cash flow:

1. *Improvements and capital expenditures.* Making improvements to the property, even if mostly cosmetic in nature, will allow you to increase the rents, improving your cash flow. If you have a capital expenditure (e.g., the property needs a new roof), you should carefully examine your ability to recoup those invested dollars and how long it will take.

2. *Lower or higher taxes and insurance.* In our estimates in the examples above, we kept the expenses at $800. However, property taxes and insurance will go up or down, depending on the value of the property. If the prior owner purchased the property ten years ago for $200,000 and we're looking at paying $600,000, the local property assessor will increase the tax-assessed value and your taxes will increase. Likewise, if we hit a bust market, you could petition the tax assessor to lower your tax-assessed value.

3. *Residential versus commercial financing.* Recall that four units and below are considered residential properties, while five units and up are considered commercial properties. The best rates and terms are for residential properties. For a complete analysis of the differences, see my earlier work, *Investing in Duplexes, Triplexes & Quads: The Fastest and Safest Way to Real Estate Wealth.* If you are willing to live in your residential property, you can get 100 percent financing from a conventional lender.

4. *Increased rents.* The goal always is to increase rents. Typically, however, this can only be done if the rents are below market or you make improvements to the property. If you can increase the rents quickly, this will affect the price you are willing to pay for the property.

5. *Location.* If the location is not great, either because it's a poor location in a city, or it is in a small town, the GRM could be as low as 3. Remember that the GRM works like comps for house sales; it really determines the fair market value. In a hot market in a hot area, and at the beach, I've

seen GRMs over 30. Where my beach condo is you can't touch anything under a GRM of 20, and most are closer to 30. And I'm not just talking about oceanfront condos. I'm including anything on the "beachside" (which means all properties on the island)—duplexes, triplexes, town homes, condos—even if they are four blocks from the beach. Needless to say, buying at a GRM of 20 or higher means you will be bleeding lots of negative cash for some time.

As you can see, you have many things to consider before making an offer on a property. Here's a short review checklist:

Investing Approach
___ Buy and hold
___ Pyramid
___ Time the market

Property Approach
___ Location/appreciation
___ Price/discount
___ Cash flow

Type of Market
___ Boom
___ Balanced
___ Bust

Other Considerations
___ Improvements and capital expenditures
___ Property taxes and insurance
___ Financing terms (especially residential v. commercial)
___ Ability to increase rents

Once you have analyzed your prospective property with these criteria and run the numbers, you should have a very good idea of whether the property will cash-flow, the amount of positive or negative cash flow, how long negative cash flow will be required, the improvements that you can make, the repairs that you need to make, when and how much you can increase rents, and your general appreciation level. Once you can gather and sift through this information, you have a formula for buying any property, regardless of size. If you are just starting out, I'd recommend staying with residential multifamily properties.

Assuming that you now have a good idea of how you'd like to invest, let's consider in Figures 7.2, 7.3, and 7.4 how each investor should proceed in any given market.

FIGURE 7.2 *Investing Actions for Buy-and-Hold Investors*

Investing Approach	Property Approach	Market	Actions
Buy and Hold	Location/ Appreciation	All	1. Always buy in great locations 2. Absorb negative cash flow 3. Pay going prices
	Price/ Discount	Boom and Balanced	1. Cannot buy in hot markets; must buy on outskirts of town or in small cities 2. Aim to buy at 15–20% under value
		Bust	1. Buy at 15–20% under value in good locations
	Cash Flow	Boom	1. Will be difficult to buy now and get cash flow; will need to search in outskirts of town and in small cities 2. Usually will need 3–4 units to see positive cash flow
		Balanced	1. If it's not a hot area of town, should be able to find a 3- to 4-unit property that will cash-flow
		Bust	1. Should be able to cash-flow in most locations; may be able to cash-flow in outstanding locations

FIGURE 7.3 *Investing Actions for Pyramid Investors*

Investing Approach	Property Approach	Market	Actions
Pyramid	Location/ Appreciation	Boom	1. Sell as soon as you have rehabbed and increased rents to capture highest price. Make sure you've held it one year to avoid being taxed as ordinary income. Buy again in great location. Rolling all of your gain (and equity) into this second property should eliminate negative cash flow.
		Balanced	1. When buying, must accept negative cash flow; appreciation will be good to great 2. Hold property 1–3 years, sell, and buy a larger property in another good location
		Bust	1. Buy, buy, buy 2. Appreciation will be slow; will need to wait until market recovers to sell
	Price/Discount	Boom and Balanced	1. Must buy on outskirts of town or in small cities 2. Try to buy at 15–20% of value 3. If discount deals can't be found, put this money into improving the properties you have
		Bust	1. Buy, buy, buy 2. Will not be able to sell quickly; must wait until market recovers to sell
	Cash Flow	Boom and Balanced	1. Will be difficult to buy now and get cash flow; will need to search in outskirts of town and in small cities 2. Usually will need 3–4 units to cash-flow 3. Sell in order to pyramid up if the gain and equity from the first property applied down on the second will give you positive cash flow
		Bust	1. Should be able to buy most anywhere and get good cash flow (less in great locations) 2. Don't sell anything now; consider pulling equity from one property to buy more

FIGURE 7.4 *Investing Actions for Time the Market Investors*

Investing Approach	Property Approach	Market	Actions
Time the Market	All	Boom	1. Sell, sell, sell 2. Must look in other real estate categories or other (non-boom) markets for any possible buying opportunities
		Balanced	1. Look for buying opportunities 2. Sell only if you get an outrageous offer
		Bust	1. Buy, buy, buy 2. Appreciation will be slow; will need to wait until market recovers to sell

Once you have determined which investing and property selection methods you prefer, start buying. Get the appreciation clock rolling. Even if prices remain flat for a while, you'll still receive excellent tax benefits (depreciation, interest deduction) and will gain valuable experience. By the time you read this, prices will have taken a hit and will have corrected downward in most areas of the country. This should be a great time for you to buy.

8

ADDITIONAL STRATEGIES FOR DIFFERENT MARKETS

If my analysis of the data is correct, 2007 (and possibly 2008) will be largely a correcting market. For single-family homes, most areas will stay relatively flat in prices, while many will drop 5 to 10 percent. A few may drop 15 percent and a few may gain 15 percent. For multifamily properties, prices came down in 2006 and may come down a bit more in 2007. Your strategies for working in a correcting market are basically the same as working in a bust market. You want to be buying. Your downside is that neither you nor I can predict the exact bottom of the market. As long as you plan to improve the property and hold it for a couple of years, you should be fine. Just make sure the numbers work in your favor regarding cash flow. It doesn't matter if the market drops another 10 percent after you buy it; that doesn't change your mortgage payment or your rents (I recommend a fixed-rate mortgage, by the way). Now let's discuss some additional things to keep in mind as you contemplate buying in 2007, 2008, and maybe 2009 (for those of you who have to see the market rising before you'll jump in).

STRATEGIES FOR INVESTING IN A BUST OR CORRECTING MARKET

Be More Aggressive with Your Leverage

In a bust or correcting market, many investors will be scared away. Some will be gone from the market entirely because they overleveraged themselves during the boom, many with adjustable-rate mortgage loans that have increased in payment amounts. You'll have fewer buyers with which to compete. You have both time and leverage on your side. Use it.

Hopefully, you have been watching your market to see what prices have been doing. In most areas, prices have been flat or dropping. Look for the motivated seller. You may see that some sellers are still clinging to the prices that were relevant in 2005. Most of them will be holding their properties for some time. Others need to sell soon, for whatever reason. Once a property sits on the market for six months to a year, sellers get the point and usually start dropping the price. The longer it sits on the MLS (multiple listing service), the more the price comes down.

Your broker can tell you how long a property has been on the market. You may also want to ask your broker if it was listed earlier and the listing agreement expired. For example, most residential listing agreements are for six or seven months. After a listing expires, it disappears from the MLS. The seller may wait another six months before listing it again. It gives you additional information and leverage if you know how long it sat on the market before, and at what price it was listed.

After you put in what you think is a fair offer, don't be in a rush to counter the seller's first counteroffer. Time is on your side, and so is supply. You should have a number of properties from which to choose. As Donald Trump says, if you really want to speed up a deal (meaning get the seller closer to your terms), ignore the seller for a while. Be unavailable.

Consider Asking for Seller Financing

You may also want to ask the seller for some financing. That is, you might ask the seller to take back a second mortgage. Most lenders will give you a first mortgage for 80 percent of the fair market value (normally seen as the purchase price). Typically, for investment property you provide the other 20 percent of the purchase price as a down payment. However, many lenders will allow the seller to take back a mortgage because the bank's mortgage will be in first position, ahead of the seller's mortgage. Many lenders will allow the seller to finance 10 percent, meaning you now only have to put down 10 percent. During a boom, as long as interest rates are low, sellers have no motivation for doing this and generally won't do it. Your opportunity to use this additional financing is now!

It should be obvious to you at this point but I'll say it anyway: the less you put down, the more risk you have of negative cash flow and losing equity if the market continues in a downward spiral. Just make sure the numbers work now, and add in a cushion if you are wrong on the numbers or have unexpected expenses or vacancies. Indeed, just expect unexpected expenses!

Consider Getting a HELOC

You may have already done this, but I would get an appraisal on whatever properties you have now. In all likelihood, if you've owned a property for several years, the appraisal numbers will be good, notwithstanding the correction. You will have acquired much equity from the great appreciation in 2004 and 2005. If you refinance or get a home equity line of credit (HELOC), the bank will usually pay the $300 to $450 for the appraisal.

I think HELOCs are a great idea for two reasons. First, if you are nervous about a bad correction, crash, or a local economy bust and think you might lose your job or tenants, a HELOC will give you ready cash if you need it. A HELOC is much better than a home equity loan (HEL). With a home equity loan, you must take out a specific amount now, pay closing costs on it such as documentary stamps, and pay it back over a fixed period of time.

Second, a HELOC gives you flexibility for buying other properties. Let's say you had $100,000 available to you to take out in a HELOC or HEL. But you just wanted to use $10,000 now for improving your house, and $30,000 later for buying a triplex, and maybe another $30,000 after that for a duplex. With a home equity loan, you don't have that luxury. You have to take it all out now, and begin paying interest on it. So you would be taking out $70,000 now and paying closing costs and interest on it even though you aren't going to be using most of it now. Good for the bank, bad for you.

Your better option is to use a HELOC. Remember that it's a line of credit. You only pull out what you need. That is, you pull out only $10,000 now for your home improvement. Six months later, when you are ready to buy that triplex, you can pull out the $30,000. Banks will either let you pay only the interest on what you pull out, or amortize each draw for up to 15 years. The beauty of having access to HELOC money is that it's there whenever you need it if you find a great deal. Besides, because it's a loan, the interest is also deductible on your taxes. Again, just make sure that you can handle the increased payment.

Consider Getting Other Investors

If the market gives you great prices, buy as much as you can. Take what the market gives you. Prices will not stay low forever. Once you've tapped out your personal resources for down payments on one or two properties, you are probably done unless you can get other investors. I have investment partners in some of my deals. You probably know many people who would love to invest in real estate but don't have the time or experience. You can give them a nice return while you increase your leverage for more of your own deals.

Deals with investors are structured many ways. In almost all cases, the investor is passive. In fact, for limited partnerships and certain tax benefits, the investor *must* be passive. That's good news for you because you don't want the investor in your hair all the time. As Warren Buffett told his first investors: "See me at the end of the year. I don't want you to see me shank one off the tee here and hit a three iron shot into the woods there. I just want to turn in a score card at the end of the year."

Most deals work in one of two ways. If you are investing in small deals (under $1 million) with one or two investors, the structure typically looks something like this: The investor is either guaranteed a specified return (such as 8 percent) or given a preference (i.e., paid first) of that return. Typically, the investor is paid that interest monthly or quarterly. After that, the managing partner (you) either gets a set management fee or a similar payment to what the investor(s) just received. When the property is sold, the investors are paid back their principal, and any gains (i.e., profits) are distributed according to ownership or by a set formula. In partnerships with several limited partners, typically the managing partner will get anywhere from 0 to 25 percent of the net proceeds until the limited partners (passive investors) are paid all of their principal and interest, and after that the managing partner gets anywhere from 50 to 90 percent of the profits and the limited partners receive 10 to 50 percent.

For larger deals ($1 million and up), the "sponsor" (you) typically would get an acquisition fee of 2 to 4 percent of the purchase price, a small management fee of 1 to 5 percent of collected rents, and a disposition fee of 2 to 5 percent upon the sale of the property. When it's all said and done, the investor should get an overall return somewhere between 15 and 25 percent on his or her original investment—without any liability risk (i.e., they never sign guarantees on loans of the partnership), of course. If the limited partners want a better return than that, they should be doing their own deals, and taking the proportional risk.

If you do choose to bring in investors, hire a securities attorney to prepare the appropriate legal documents. The disclosure and information requirements vary depending on the amount of money you are raising and whether you are bringing in any unaccredited investors. An *accredited investor* under the Securities and Exchange Commission laws is someone who has a net worth of over $1 million, or has made $200,000 in each of the past two years (or at least $300,000 with their spouse). You will also need to let your attorney know if you will have any investors who live in other states, because the attorney must review and comply with the "blue sky" laws in those states as well.

In general, your attorney will prepare a disclosure questionnaire for your investors to complete, and a private placement memorandum (PPM) to give them. The questionnaire is given to them to find out whether they are accredited, and to have a record of that fact if they are. The PPM sets forth not only the terms of the deal, but also the appropriate legal disclosures that must be made under federal and state laws.

A word of caution: Don't try to sell your deal in this PPM. It's not a sales brochure. It's a legal disclosure document. I can't tell you how many clients have asked me, "How can I sell this to my investors? You make it sound like a horrible investment." I always tell them that the investors expect this kind of document. Sell your prospective investors over lunch at a nice restaurant. The PPM should err on the side of caution. Don't be alarmed when you see that your attorney has written things that would seem to scare investors away, such as, "You could lose your entire investment." Sophisticated investors not only expect such language, but they will expect to see such disclosures if they have participated in many deals with PPMs prepared by securities attorneys. The absence of them would raise a red flag because it would reveal that you did the PPM in-house because you either didn't know better or you couldn't afford an attorney. In either case, that's bad and you'll scare the investor away.

If possible, try to get a referral to a securities attorney. If you can't get a referral, contact the local bar association in your area, which typically will give you a list of attorneys by area of practice. Most large law firms will have someone who practices in this area.

Consider Refinancing an Existing Property

The strategy of refinancing an existing property really applies to bust, balanced, or correcting markets. If prices are great, or simply fair, you can buy new properties by pulling cash out of existing properties. Ideally, you refinance from a higher interest rate to a lower interest rate, from an adjustable rate to a fixed rate, or from an interest-only rate to a fully amortized loan. That way you are killing two birds with one stone; you are improving your financing on an existing property while acquiring cash to buy another property.

One word of caution here: Be careful that your new mortgage payment doesn't exceed your rents. When you refinance and pull cash out to buy another property, your loan balance increases and, unless you have lowered your interest rate or increased your amortization period, your monthly payment will increase. If you are thinking about refinancing, you should have increased the rents since you bought the property—either from improvements or simply because you've owned it for years and the rents have gone up over time.

Foreclosures and Pre-foreclosures

I personally do not invest in foreclosures or pre-foreclosure deals, but many investors do. And the market for working in this area could not be better. Because bank lending has been so aggressive over the past few years, with many adjustable-rate and interest-only mortgages, many home and property owners are losing their properties to foreclosure.

In September 2006 alone, 112,000 U.S. single-family homes fell into foreclosure. That's a 63 percent jump from a year earlier. Three Web sites that specialize in advertising foreclosure investing are Foreclosure.com, RealtyTrac.com, and PropertyShark.com. In Chapter 10, I'll give the top ten markets for investing in foreclosures.

Tax Deed Sales

With a correcting real estate market, and especially with a bust market, the number of properties being sold at tax deed sales is likely to increase. A tax deed sale is when a local property tax jurisdiction (typically the county) conducts a public sale of a property for failure of the owner to pay property taxes. This is the only method of which I know where an investor can literally buy a property for pennies on the dollar. I purchased a house once (needing a ton of work) for $4,100 and I've purchased residential lots for $75. But let me state clearly, those kinds of buys are extremely rare.

Notwithstanding what you'll hear on late-night and weekend infomercials, very few property owners will let their properties go for just the back taxes, amounting to only pennies on the dollar. I've been to tax lien and deed sales in about 15 states and this kind of thing is very rare. What is far more common is for a county to sell a tax deed or lien on a worthless property. In my experience, most good properties sold at tax deed auctions sell for about 50 cents on the dollar. When I say "good," I mean that it is a lot that you can build on, or a property that has a building that doesn't have to be torn down. If this area interests you, see my first book, *Profit by Investing in Real Estate Tax Liens: Earn Safe, Secured, and Fixed Returns Every Time.* I cover both tax liens and deeds in this book.

One other cautionary note regarding tax liens and tax deeds: They are never—I repeat, *never*—"guaranteed" by the county or any other jurisdiction. I have seen books and heard many a speaker touting that you can buy liens with a "guaranteed" 16 percent, 18 percent, or 50 percent return. Nothing could be further from the truth, as anyone who has been to a sale can testify. In fact, most counties state very clearly *"caveat emptor"* (buyer beware) on their auction literature. Not only that, but counties regularly sell liens on ditches, utility encumbered properties, and deeds on unbuildable lots. Having said all of that, you can get a nice passive return on liens, and can pick up some cheap properties (95 percent are vacant lots) with tax deeds. See my previous book for further study.

ADDITIONAL STRATEGIES FOR ANY MARKET

Become a Licensed REALTOR®

Most states distinguish between a REALTOR®, or real estate sales associate, and a broker. The latter carries legal implications and more stringent requirements, while the former can be acquired fairly easily with a class and state exam. In Florida, for example, one must take a class and pass a test to become a REALTOR®, or sales associate. This individual must hang his or her license with a licensed broker. After one year, if the associate desires to also become a broker, he or she must take another class and take another test. While you don't need a broker license, I would encourage you to get a REALTOR® license so that you can participate in the listing broker's commission when you buy.

In most cases, a seller lists a property for sale with a REALTOR®
(who works under a broker) or broker. The listing agreement
will establish a real estate commission to be paid upon the sale
of the property. In most instances for residential property, that
commission is 5 to 7 percent (it could be as low as 1 or 2 percent for a large commercial property). If the listing agent finds a
buyer on his or her own, that agent gets all of the commission. If
another agent brings in the buyer (which happens in most cases),
the two agents split the commission. As such, if the commission is
6 percent, each agent receives 3 percent (less what their supervis-
ing broker, if applicable, may take).

If you are buying a property and you happen to be a real estate
agent, you can still capture this commission. That's sort of like having your cake and eating it too. Assume that you are buying a triplex for $400,000 and the listing agreement sets forth a 6 percent
real estate commission. Your half of that, 3 percent, is $12,000!
That will go a long way in assisting you with the down payment.

Buy a Quad and Live in the Property

While I covered this topic in detail in my previous book, let me
just summarize here why this is a great idea. If you can buy a quad
(four units), or even a triplex if a quad is not available, you will
capture many benefits. First, even a four-unit apartment building
is considered "residential" for loan purposes. As such, you get the
absolute best financing. In fact, if you will live in the property, you
can get 100 percent financing. Since it qualifies as a personal residence, you can claim and file for a homestead exemption, which
will lower your property taxes.

Second, you have less risk with a quad, as I've mentioned
earlier. If you have a vacancy, your overall expenses should still
be either totally covered, or mostly covered, by the other tenants.
Moreover, when prices start to creep up, you, as one willing to live
in one of the units, will have an overwhelming advantage over your

competition. Understand that very few homeowners want to buy a triplex or quad as their "home." They want a single-family home. That leaves only real estate investors as your competition. But, since they have their own single-family home somewhere else they must buy the property as an "investment" property. As such, their lender will generally want 20 percent down, they will get a higher interest rate, and they will pay more in property taxes. Therefore, you would have a built-in advantage over them in what you could pay for the property and still break even or see a positive cash flow. It's not for everyone, but if you need a bootstrap method to break into this game, this is it.

C h a p t e r

9

CRASH, CORRECTION, OR COOLING? WHAT IS COMING?

Having pointed out the dangers of trying to predict the future in Chapter 2, I want to be very careful about playing the prognosticator. Many bright people spend a great deal of time trying to predict markets (e.g., real estate, stock, futures, oil, etc.) and are often wrong. But I would be remiss if this book on investing in boom or bust markets didn't devote some space to where I think the real estate market is going. The problem, of course (if you've been paying attention), is *which* market? The market in San Francisco? New York? Peoria? Due South (yes, just ask the folks in South Carolina, this is a real city)?

To know a market really well, you need to live there. You need to review the newspaper daily for things such as employment, construction starts, migration of residents, job growth, properties on the market, GRM rates (for residential multifamily), cap rates (for commercial properties), and so on. This takes time and I only do it for my hometown, Orlando (which has one of the lowest unemployment rates in the country and is very high in "in-migration"). As such, I'll rely on statistics produced by others such as the National Association of Realtors®, Harvard University, Fiserv Lending Solutions, Moody's Economy.com, National City Corp., Global Insight, *Business 2.0* magazine, *SmartMoney* magazine, RealtyTrak, RealEstateJournal.com, Dataquick, and CNNMoney.com, and try to give my overall thoughts to investing in other areas.

WILL THERE BE A NATIONAL REAL ESTATE CRASH?

I'm not an economist or a futurist, but I don't think we'll see a true real estate crash this decade. The few authors predicting a real estate crash have been wrong so far. Will there be a correction in the market? Of course. We've already seen that.

On October 25, 2006, the National Association of Realtors® reported the biggest drop in home prices since the group started collecting price data in 1968. The trade association reported specifically that the median home price in September 2006 was down 2.2 percent from a year earlier. On October 26, 2006, the Commerce Department reported that *new* home prices fell in September 2006 by 9.7 percent from September 2005, the largest decline in 35 years. The report stated that the median price of a U.S. home was $217,000, down from $240,000 a year earlier. This finding on new home sales came on the heels of a report by the agency on October 25, 2006, stating that prices on sales of *existing* homes had decreased 2.5 percent from a year earlier. This seems like a small drop but it was the largest drop in existing home sale prices in nearly 40 years.

So real estate markets were correcting in 2006 and likely will continue to do so in 2007 and possibly 2008. Naples, which was one of the hottest markets in the boom, saw price declines of 15 to 20 percent from their 2005 peak to the third quarter in 2006.[1] But some markets stayed relatively flat in 2006, and some even saw price increases. For example, the median price in Seattle as of September 2006 was *up* 9.4 percent from a year earlier. The median home price in the eight-county region of Charlotte, North Carolina, was up 6 percent in the third quarter of 2006 from a year earlier. The median home price in California was up 7 percent in 2006. Houston prices were also up.[2]

On the other hand, some have suggested that house prices could fall more than 10 percent from their peak in places such as Sacramento, San Diego, Las Vegas, Reno, Phoenix, and parts of northern Virginia and Florida.[3] But these corrections will be market specific. One market might see a 10 percent drop in 2006 and a 5 percent gain in 2007. Another market might see an 8 percent gain in 2006 and a 12 percent drop in 2007. I can tell you what won't happen; we won't see a uniform decline of 15 percent in every market in America. See Appendix B for a forecast of 25 major markets.

But what does this mean? Does it suggest that the correction is just starting or almost over? Does it suggest that a crash is yet to come? Again, it depends on how we define a "crash," but few, if any, cities should expect to see declines in home prices of over 20 percent. If we define a crash as a price decline of 10 percent or more, we may see a few cities hit that mark. According to the National Association of REALTORS®, median existing home prices are expected to rise 1.7 percent in 2007, while new home prices are expected to rise 1.3 percent.[4] David Seiders, chief economist of the National Association of Home Builders, predicts that home prices overall (new and existing) will increase 4.4 percent in 2007.[5] Remember that these figures are national and averages, which means that some markets may gain 5 to 10 percent and some markets may lose 5 to 10 percent.

We also have to decide how to measure—year to year, or from the highest price peak to the lowest bottom? One thing is certain: Numerous markets will see slight price drops in 2007. But how many cities, which cities, and how severe and how long the decline will last is the question.

WHAT FACTORS SUGGEST THAT THERE WILL *NOT* BE A REAL ESTATE CRASH?

Do we have any guarantees that any particular market will not see a 20 to 30 percent drop in median home prices, as some have predicted? No. But we have plenty of evidence that this kind of a crash is highly unlikely (absent major job losses in a market due to a major employer leaving or closing a plant). Here are some major reasons why I think a national real estate crash is unlikely.

Historically Low Mortgage Rates and a Strong Economy Will Continue

In 2004, the chief economists of the top five leading organizations in the nation met to discuss the future of the housing market. The organizations were the National Association of REALTORS®, Fannie Mae, Freddie Mac, National Association of Home Builders, and America's Community Bankers Association. The group provided a 10-year projection of the housing market, forecasting annual appreciation in the 5 to 6 percent range over that time span. In other words, they projected appreciation very near to the 35-year annual average of 6.7 percent. The group suggested that the stability and continued growth of the real estate market was based on many factors, including:

- Mortgage rates are forecast to stay in the 5.5 to 8.5 percent range for the remainder of this decade.
- Today's economic expansion is expected to create healthy job and income gains for the remainder of the decade.
- Home price appreciation will continue due to a lean inventory of homes.
- New projections based on the 2000 Census suggest stronger than anticipated household growth.

- The baby boomer population will age into their peak earn-ing years, creating greater demand for second homes.
- The baby boomers' children—the echo generation—will be entering home-buying age.
- The large retiree population will live longer due to advances in health care, creating additional demand for retirement and vacation homes.
- Minority home ownership rates will continue to rise during the next decade.[6]

Take a look at the average 30-year mortgage rates in Figure 9.1. As of this writing, we are hovering around 6.36 percent for a fixed, fully amortized loan. As you can see from the chart, this puts us among the lowest mortgage rates in the past 34 years or so.

As an investor, I'm willing to pay more for a property with these low rates because my mortgage payment will be low, allow-ing for positive monthly cash flow (or less negative cash flow). If rates were at 9 percent, for example, it would be very difficult to see the annual double-digit price increases, at least for rental properties, because many properties would begin to see negative cash flow at current prices.

Household Growth and Graying Baby Boomers

In June 2006, the Harvard Joint Center for Housing Studies (JCHS) released a report finding that the housing market was entering a down cycle, but that it was unlikely to undergo a severe reversal. Nicholas Retsinas, director of Harvard's JCHS, stated at the time that "[t]here may be tough times ahead, but housing will emerge stronger than ever." While Retsinas stated that some areas might be more susceptible to a slide, the study concluded that any softening in the housing market would firm up and that home demand and prices would remain healthy. The Center noted the following factors in its findings:

FIGURE 9.1 *Thirty-Year Mortgage Rates*

Year	30-Year Rate	Year	30-Year Rate
1972	7.38%	1990	10.13%
1973	8.09	1991	9.23
1974	9.19	1992	8.40
1975	9.04	1993	7.33
1976	8.86	1994	8.36
1977	8.84	1995	7.96
1978	9.63	1996	7.81
1979	11.19	1997	7.60
1980	13.77	1998	6.94
1981	16.63	1999	7.43
1982	16.08	2000	8.06
1983	13.23	2001	6.97
1984	13.87	2002	6.54
1985	12.42	2003	5.82
1986	10.18	2004	5.84
1987	10.20	2005	5.87
1988	10.34	2006*	6.36
1989	10.32		

* Rate as of October 19, 2006
Source: Freddie Mac Primary Market Survey, in David Lereah, *Why the Real Estate Boom Will Not Bust—And How You Can Profit From It* (Currency Doubleday, 2005)

- The strong U.S. economy
- Booming household growth (1.37 million new households in 2006)
- Graying boomers (creating more demand for second and vacation homes)
- Changing household composition (i.e., more single-person households, increases in divorce rates) creating more demand for housing
- Increasing homeownership among minorities

- Increased government regulation on building (i.e., land-use restrictions, zoning laws, and building codes) restricting an increase in the supply of housing

Stability of the High Volume of Mortgage Applications

Perhaps no other person in America has been more respected in reporting or influencing the recent housing boom than former Federal Reserve Chairman, Alan Greenspan. In fact, it was Greenspan's interest rate cuts that helped usher in the boom and create what he later called "froth" in housing prices. However, in a speech to the Commercial Finance Association on October 26, 2006, Greenspan stated that he saw "early signs of stabilization" in the housing market. One sign he noted was that a weekly index of mortgage applications, compiled by the Mortgage Bankers Association, had flattened at relatively high prices.[7]

Economists Predict a Rebound in 2008

We have seen a correction in home prices for 2006. More corrections will come in 2007 as the buyers and sellers adjust supply and demand. By 2008, I think we'll see a rebound of home prices. Mark Zandi, chief economist at Moody's Economy.com reported on October 27, 2006, that "[t]he housing market correction is in full swing, but it probably has another year to go before it bottoms out."[8] Zandi predicts a 3.7 percent price decline for existing homes for 2007, which would be the first such decline for a full year since the Great Depression.

Gregory Miller, chief economist at SunTrust Banks in Atlanta, doesn't expect single-family home prices to resume their usual rising trend until 2008.[9] Peter Kretzmer, a senior economist at Bank of America in New York, expects gradual improvement from the third quarter of 2006 on. He forecasts a 5 percent decline in residential construction in the first quarter of 2007 and a 2.2 percent decline in the second quarter before starting to grow again in the third quarter of 2007.[10] Ivy Zelman, a housing analyst for Credit Suisse in Cleveland who correctly predicted in 2005 the plunge in homebuilder stock prices, suggests that sales of new homes are unlikely to start rising again until 2008.[11]

On November 6, 2006, former Fed chairman Alan Greenspan stated that the U.S. housing market would weaken further, but that the sharpest decline was over as inventories of unsold homes decreased. Said Greenspan, "This is not the bottom, but the worst is behind us."[12]

In November 2006, a report by Metrostudy also hinted that the housing market might turn around by mid-2007. Metrostudy President Mike Inselmann cautioned that the market first had to hit the bottom of the cycle, but suggested several factors indicating a turnaround, including:

- Strong new job creation
- Low unemployment in many U.S. cities
- Cutbacks in new home production
- The exit of most residential real estate investors
- Fundamental demographic support for housing
- The Federal Reserve Board curtailing its series of rate increases
- A drop in mortgage rates in late 2006[13]

To be fair and balanced, of course, I want to include forecasts from the bears as well. Jack McCabe, CEO of McCabe Research and Consulting, believes that home prices will drop in 2007 and 2008.[14] Joshua Shapiro, chief U.S. economist at MFR, a New York–based research firm, holds that U.S. home prices will "stagnate" for several years because price increases in some cities are offset by price declines in other markets. Shapiro states that the steep surge in prices during the first half of this decade will require time for incomes to catch up again with house prices.[15] It seems that Shapiro is hedging his bet by not specifically defining his time frame. If his "several years" is from 2006 to early 2008, his forecast would be in line with that of the other economists.

Local Nature of Real Estate Markets

As we've seen before, almost nothing happens nationally and consistently with real estate. Real estate is a local phenomenon. Will there be more price corrections in 2007 and 2008? Yes and no. In some markets, yes, we'll see 2 to 15 percent price corrections. That's a big spread. But we also can see larger spreads than that in just one market.

Consider, for example, the San Diego market, where prices have skyrocketed from 2002 to 2005. This market should have witnessed a dramatic price correction in 2006, right? Did it? Yes and no. It depends on which *part* of San Diego to which you are referring. In September 2006, the median price of a Central San Diego home was $515,000, down 5.5 percent from a year earlier. No surprise there, right? But do you think some submarkets did a little better than that, and some did a little worse? Sure. Could you have done very well (or poorly), depending on where you invested within this market?

If you are into real estate as an investment (and not as someone looking to buy a home to live in for personal enjoyment), you simply can throw out these average numbers, whether national, state, or even local. Consider this: In the period from September 2005 to September 2006, some Central San Diego submarkets were *up* 6 percent (e.g., Morena, Logan Heights), 12 percent (College), even 48 percent (Ocean Beach), while other submarkets were *down* 10 percent (Clairmont, Hillcrest, Mission Hills, Scripps Ranch), 11 percent (University City, Sorrento Valley), 12 percent (Serra Mesa, Pointe Loma), 13 percent (North Park), 16 percent (Kensington/Normal Heights), and 32 percent (Coronado).[16] Do you think it matters to the property owners in Ocean Beach (up

48 percent) or Coronado (down 32 percent) that the Central San Diego *average* was down 5.5 percent? No.

Consider the disparity in these other San Diego submarkets:

East County

Descanso	+126%
Jacumba	+17%
Alpine	+15%
Campo	−10%

North County Inland

Borrego Springs	+42%
Valley Center	+12%
Julian	+12%
Poway	−16%
Bonsall	−28%
Palomar Mountain	−32%

North County Coast

Solano Beach	+61%
Carlsbad S.	−15%
Cardiff	−26%

South County

Chula Vista SE	+19%
Chula Vista NE	−11%
San Ysidro	−13%

Can you see that someone is making money in these submarkets? Remember, these are numbers for resales of existing homes, not new home sales. Some investors will be selling at very high prices in some of these submarkets and some will be buying at very low prices, serious discounts to the 2005 prices. This is why national and average numbers are almost meaningless to the real estate investor. Bargain hard for a good price with the statistics that you have, improve the property, increase the rent (if you are renting it out), and you will do just fine.

Having made this point about the local nature of investing, the evidence does seem to point, however, to some continued price declines in many markets and submarkets in 2007 and perhaps into 2008 for a few markets. That will create buying opportunities in these markets, just as it has in San Diego. Other markets will continue to appreciate in 2007 and 2008 and beyond, just at a slower pace. Amidst the price declines, for example, the Panama City market is expected to appreciate 21 percent from 2006 to 2007, and 72 percent through 2011. And again, while single-family home prices may be going down, residential multi-family dwellings, or other types of real estate, may be going up. Invest in what you know, preferably in markets that you know. You will have lots of options as prices continue to find their stability in the months ahead.

Stability of Real Estate Construction

On October 28, 2006, McGraw-Hill Construction, a forecasting subsidiary of McGraw-Hill Companies, predicted that the value of new construction will decline 1 percent in 2007, the first decline in overall construction spending since 1991. Overall construction spending increased 12 percent in 2005 and 1 percent in 2006. McGraw-Hill reported that the decrease for 2007 is due to a 5 percent decline in construction of single-family homes.[17] Two things are worth noting in this report. First, single-family home construction is predicted to be down 5 percent in 2007 (which doesn't seem too alarming), but construction of other real estate categories must be up to bring overall construction to only a decline of 1 percent. Second, considering the rising and unstable prices of construction materials over the past 12 months, this minimal decline in overall construction, while significant, is not alarming.

The Economy

Housing and the economy are inextricably linked. Some have estimated that the housing market comprises 10 percent of the U.S. economy because it involves the construction industry, the furniture and appliance industries, the mortgage industry, the household goods industry, and so on. Some economists were worried in 2005 and early 2006 that a dramatic housing slowdown would push the economy into a recession. And a weak economy or recession would result in job losses, which would depress housing prices. But that has not been the case. The economy remains strong, notwithstanding a housing retrenchment. Consider the following factors that suggest we will continue to have a strong economy and housing market in 2007 and beyond:

- Robert Brusca, economist at FAO Economics, speaking in October 2006 about the housing slowdown and its effect on the broader economy, said: "What does the GDP [gross domestic product] report say about growth ahead? I think—coupled with recent monthly indicators—it is upbeat." And, referring to the impact of the housing slowdown, Brusca added, "It's a bee sting, maybe a couple of bee stings. Yeah, it hurts, but there hasn't been the allergic reaction many feared would cause worse problems."
- On October 25, 2006, the Federal Reserve reported that "[g]oing forward, the economy seems likely to expand at a moderate pace."
- Some economists, such as Anthony Chan, chief economist at J.P. Morgan Private Client Services, expect the Fed to cut interest rates in early 2007. This notion may stem from the fact that the Federal Reserve has mentioned the cooling housing market in its last three statements as it has left interest rates unchanged after a series of 17 straight rate hikes.

- Much of the softening in the housing market stems from the overbuilding in 2005, and the large number of houses purchased by speculating investors now looking to sell. Most prior housing downturns resulted from a market's high unemployment or high interest rates. However, the national unemployment rate now is a low 4.6 percent, near its lowest in five years. And mortgage rates, currently at 6.36 percent for a 30-year fixed-rate mortgage, remain near historic lows.
- The Dow Jones Industrial Average hit historic highs in October 2006. In addition, 56 percent of the S&P 500 companies reporting as of October 2006 showed a 20.1 percent increase in earnings.[18]

Multifamily Properties

Thus far, we've been looking at the market outlook for single-family homes. Certainly, that is the biggest segment of our real estate market, but if you are a real estate investor, chances are, you are either investing in multifamily properties now or want to (and should, in my opinion, unless real estate is your full-time occupation). While multifamily properties of two to four units are considered residential properties (with five units and up being considered commercial properties), the market research earlier in this chapter only addresses single-family homes. Let's now look at the market outlook for all multifamily properties.

One of the largest brokerage firms in the commercial real estate industry is CB Richard Ellis, whom I recommended (with Cushman Wakefield) in my prior book as one of the best in the business. In just the *first two quarters* of 2006, CBRE reported $9.9 *billion* in multifamily housing sales. And these numbers are before combining numbers with Trammell Crow Co., which CBRE is scheduled to buy for $2.2 billion in the fourth quarter of 2006 or the first quarter of 2007. Combined, the conglomerate will have over 21,000 employees and offices in 50 countries, making it the world's largest commercial real estate firm. So when this company releases information on the market for multifamily housing, it's a good idea to pay attention.

In November 2006, CB Richard Ellis held its sixth annual Multi-Housing Outlook in Hollywood, Florida. While CBRE will represent buyers and sellers in the commercial multifamily property industry (generally with properties valued at $1 million and up), the research and findings revealed at their November conference will generally apply to all multifamily properties. For example, if you own a quad, your rents will likely compete with the 30-unit apartment building down the street. Here, then, are the more significant findings released at this Outlook conference.

First, the CBRE executives predicted solid growth in employment, population, and rents in 2007. In addition, the company forecast a robust 2007 first quarter for multifamily sales. Other findings released by CBRE included:

- In 2006, lower prices and higher cap rates for multifamily properties brought back the more traditional buy-and-hold investor.
- Transactions take about 4.5 months from initial marketing to closing.
- Rental households are increasing and were estimated at 35 million for 2006.
- Average rents surpassed consumer inflation in 2006 for the first time since 2002, and with the strongest momentum since the mid-1990s.
- The price of homes is the most important factor in determining rental rates.
- Real estate, construction, and related groups accounted for 20 percent of all jobs in hot real estate markets.[19]

I trust that CBRE is accurate in its market outlook for multifamily housing. Not only must one respect this research based on the size of the company and volume of sales, this report also seems to coincide somewhat with what I've seen for single-family homes. But it appears that multifamily housing may rebound just ahead of homes. Notice that CBRE suggests a robust 2007 first quarter for multifamily property sales. As noted earlier, most economists are predicting a rebound in single-family homes anywhere from mid-2007 to early 2008. So, whether you are investing in single-family homes or multifamily properties, this looks like a good time to buy.

No doubt, money is going to be made in real estate over the next few years. Smart investors will buy properties at nice discounts in weak markets such as Dallas and Ft. Worth. They will buy properties that will appreciate well in places such as Panama City and Vero Beach. Some will invest well in multifamily properties just before prices begin to rise significantly. Others will make money in foreclosures in places such as Greeley, Colorado, and Detroit. And still others will capture quickly appreciating properties in other segments like resort properties and student housing. Will you be one of them?

10

WHERE DO I
INVEST NOW?

At this point you have to think about whether you will be in the buying mode, and, if so, in what category and in what city. In my opinion, as stated, your safest investment category is residential multifamily. You also may be able to do well buying houses, but it's just more difficult making a single-family home cash-flow if you rent it. Ideally, invest in your local market. The problem, of course, is that you may have a horrible GRM (multifamily) or overvalued houses for buying locally. In that case, you may want to check the listings on LoopNet (*www.loopnet.com*) for multifamily and commercial properties and at Realtor.com for national listings of single-family and multifamily properties. Those looking for commercial properties will want to compare cap rates in different areas. As we saw in Chapter 9, you can have a great disparity of prices even within one market. The general rule of thumb here is to know your market and buy in a good area (assuming the cash flow numbers work).

Many investors really like buying single-family homes to rehab and rent or rehab and flip. Fortunately for these investors, there's plenty of research data available on single-family homes. The question is whether you want to invest in other cities or states. If your local area isn't the best right now, and you like houses, consider buying in another market (generally, the closer the better). I've owned houses in other states, and there are certainly some obvious disadvantages. You can't visit it every week to see how the tenants are keeping it up. You can't check on the yard every week to see if the yard person is doing the job.

As such, if you buy in another area, you'll want to hire a good property manager. I've used RE/MAX for management before and found their managers professional and reliable. I remember a call I got from my RE/MAX property manager a number of years ago on a house I owned in Memphis: "Um, Larry . . . you're not going to believe this, but somebody ran into your house." "You mean jogging?" I replied. "No, I mean they drove their car into your house!" Yikes! (Not the word I said then.) Fortunately, it was a block (as opposed to wood frame) house and little real damage was done. So, if you decide to buy out of your area, get a good property manager. A manager will generally want about 10 percent of the collected rents to manage it for you, and will also charge you a separate fee to show and rent the house if it's vacant.

WHERE TO BUY A HOUSE

On June 12, 2006, National City Corp., a financial holding company, and Global Insight, a financial information company, released a study indicating the most overvalued and undervalued housing markets in the United States. If, as Warren Buffett says, price is what you pay but value is what you get, the study's findings are worth noting. Surveying the 317 largest U.S. cities, the report estimated what home prices should be, adjusting for differences in population, income levels, interest rates, and historical market premiums or discounts. The top five undervalued markets were all in Texas—College Station, Dallas, Ft. Worth, Houston, and Killeen. These are the levels of under valuation:

Area	Median Price (Q1, 2006)	Percent Undervalued (Q1, 2006)
1. College Station	$ 94,200	23.7%
2. Dallas	$129,000	18.9%
3. Ft. Worth	$105,500	18.5%
4. Houston	$110,600	15.8%
5. Killeen	$ 93,000	15.1%

On July 13, 2006, *Money* magazine reported a study of 380 markets by forecasters at Fiserv Lending Solutions and Moody's Economy.com to predict what each market will do in the period from June 2006 to June 2007. While much of this short window of time may have passed by the time you read this, these markets should continue to be strong, probably well into 2008 or beyond. The forecasters predict the following top ten appreciating housing markets for June 2006 through June 2007:

1. Panama City, FL	21%
2. Wenatchee, WA (about 150 miles southeast of Seattle)	16%
3. Mount Vernon, WA	14%
4. El Centro, CA	14%
5. Lakeland, FL	14%
6. Olympia, WA	13%
7. Ocala, FL	13%
8. Yakima, WA	13%
9. Spokane, WA	12%
10. Flagstaff, AZ	12%

On October 25, 2006, *Business 2.0* magazine, using research from Moody's Economy.com and others, released its own top-ten list of places to buy houses. This list, however, projected a *five-year* gain. Only two cities came in the top ten in both lists—Panama City, Florida (at number one on both lists) and Lakeland, Florida. Here's the top ten based on a five-year projection (2006–2011) of appreciation:

1.	Panama City, FL	72%
2.	Vero Beach, FL	64%
3.	Bridgeport, CN	63%
4.	Lakeland, FL	59%
5.	McAllen, TX	57%
6.	San Luis Obispo, CA	40%
7.	Wilmington, NC	37%
8.	Manchester, NH	35%
9.	Ft. Collins, CO	28%
10.	Atlanta, GA	24%

WHY THESE CITIES?

Let's look at how and why *Business 2.0* picked these cities. Even if you are not interested in investing in houses in these cities, pay attention to the demographic, development, and business factors that contributed to their inclusion in the top ten list. You can apply them to your city and the surrounding areas.

Panama City, Florida

Projected single-family home appreciation over five years: 72%

Median home price:
2006 $223,000
2011 $383,000

Population:
2006   166,000
2011   187,000

Per capita income:
2006 $31,000
2011 $40,200

Key information:
- St. Joe, one of the largest real estate developers in the country, is planning to build, together with state and local government agencies, a new airport by 2008 at a cost of over $300 million. Local officials expect the airport to increase attraction to the area the way that Southwest Florida International Airport helped drive a housing boom in Ft. Myers and surrounding areas in the 1980s.
- House prices are still low by Florida standards and the local market already absorbed a price correction after peaking in 2005.
- Two-bedroom beachfront condos can still be acquired for as little as $330,000, down $100,000 from 2005.

Caution: Local officials have approved several master-plan communities. If too much supply is built, prices will stall.

Personal note: Panama City Beach is known to have one of the nicest beaches in the world. I've vacationed at a smaller beach just north of there, in Destin, Florida. Both beaches are wide, clean, and have lily white, soft sand.

Vero Beach, Florida

Projected single-family home appreciation over five years: 64%

Median home price:
2006 $235,000
2011 $386,000

Population:
2006   131,000
2011   147,000

Per capita income:
2006 $44,400
2011 $51,200

Key information:
- A recent Florida Atlantic University study projected that Indian River County (where Vero Beach is located) and its two closest counties will need 154,000 new homes over the next 25 years.
- A Manpower Employment Outlook Survey predicts job growth in construction, manufacturing, and retail.
- Per capita income growth for Vero Beach closely tracks Martin County (which includes Hutchinson Beach, Jensen Beach, Jupiter Island, and Stuart, Florida), Florida's second wealthiest county (behind only Palm Beach County).

Caution: Job growth is projected to be mostly in lower-wage work, which could hurt home appreciation. Steven Cochrane, chief regional economist for Moody's Economy.com, states, "Vero Beach is at high risk in the short term but will move up in the long term."[1]

Personal note: Vero Beach has been somewhat of a sleeping giant in Florida. A Fortune 500 company (Harris) is headquartered just north of Vero in Melbourne, and several attractive areas lie just south of Vero (Hutchinson Island, Jensen Beach, Jupiter Island).

Bridgeport, Connecticut

Projected single-family home appreciation over five years: 63%

Median home price:
2006 $480,000
2011 $784,000

Population:
2006   910,000
2011   934,000

Per capita income:
2006 $70,000
2011 $87,000

Key information:
- While *Business 2.0* lists the median home price at $480,000, it lists the average home price at a depressed $280,000. Compare that with the county's other large urban area, Stamford, which has an average home price of $840,000. As a result of the drastic price differential, many entry-level professionals are moving to Bridgeport to take advantage of bargain prices.
- Prior political corruption has apparently been cleansed and the new officials are pro-development.

Caution: Because Bridgeport doesn't have much of a local economy, housing prices are largely controlled by the health of New York's business.

Lakeland, Florida

Projected single-family home appreciation over five years: 59%

Median home price:
2006 $178,000
2011 $282,000

Population:
2006   551,000
2011   599,000

Per capita income:
2006 $30,200
2011 $39,100

Key information:
- A house in Lakeland sells for well under the national median price of $227,500 and is only 30 minutes from Tampa, a metropolitan area of 2.7 million people that is expected to add an additional 210,000 residents over the next five years.
- Lakeland sits along the Interstate 4 corridor, connecting Orlando to Tampa, where the density of development is beginning to mirror the Dulles corridor in Virginia.

Caution: Prices tend to peak quickly in markets like Lakeland, where most of the workers are semiskilled service employees.

Personal note: I have done some real estate shopping in Lakeland myself. The prices are no doubt low, both for houses and residential multifamily. I've been keeping an eye on it. It's about an hour's drive from Orlando; just a bit farther than I want to drive. But it's one of the last places to get decent prices in a Florida metropolitan market. I've worried over the last few years about appreciation there, but it may in fact be on the verge of taking off.

McAllen, Texas

Projected single-family home appreciation over five years: 57%

Median home price:
2006 $ 70,000
2011 $109,000

Population:
2006   695,000
2011   785,000

Per capita income:
2006 $17,000
2011 $23,200

Key information:
- McAllen is located on the southern tip of Texas, just across the border from Mexico. Its residents are 85 percent Latino, whose average family size is 3.8 members (compared with 2.4 for Caucasians). Steven Cochrane, chief regional economist for Moody's Economy.com, states: "These border towns have a housing shortage. There's pent-up demand. They'll be looking for more space and better space."
- Cheap labor has driven a development boom. In part due to NAFTA, manufacturers locate on both sides of the border to take advantage of low wages and the common market for goods.

Caution: As the economy in McAllen grows, higher-paying industries like health care and business services could dilute the "cheap labor" edge, slowing down economic growth and the demand for new housing.

San Luis Obispo, California

Projected single-family home appreciation over five years: 40%

Median home price:
2006 $440,000
2011 $615,000

Population:
2006   261,000
2011   287,000

Per capita income:
2006 $34,400
2011 $42,900

Key information:
- San Luis Obispo (SLO) sits in the middle of the last semirural central California coastline and is becoming a rising star in wine production. Even French vintners are buying property in SLO's Paso Robles, where median home prices have jumped over 100 percent since 2000. Commercial land has jumped from $3 per square foot to $20 since 2001. Antidevelopment sentiment will help to drive up prices.
- SLO's proximity to Southern California and low prices may draw thousands of retiring baby boomers.

Caution: Prices are already exceeding job and income growth.

Wilmington, North Carolina

Projected single-family home appreciation over five years: 37%

Median home price:
2006 $217,000
2011 $297,000

Population:
2006   325,000
2011   361,000

Per capita income:
2006 $30,500
2011 $38,300

Key information:
- Wilmington has great golf, mild seasons, natural beauty, and a relatively cheap cost of living, all of which make it popular for local and second home residents.
- Wilmington has a seaport, an international airport, and a University of North Carolina campus. In addition, its "historic" ambiance has led Hollywood to film 180 movies here over the past 20 years.

Caution: Wilmington has its share of speculating investors. *Barron's* estimated in 2005 that 38 percent of its homeowners are nonresident investors who only rarely use their properties. The other caution is hurricanes.

Manchester, New Hampshire

Projected single-family home appreciation over five years: 35%

Median home price:
2006 $226,000
2011 $305,000

Population:
2006   404,000
2011   413,000

Per capita income:
2006 $41,500
2011 $54,200

Key information:
- New Hampshire has no income or sales tax, and Manchester is within commuting distance to Boston, one of the most expensive housing markets in the country. Neighboring city Nashua has twice won the honors as *Money* magazine's "best place to live" in America.
- Housing appreciation rates started falling in New England several quarters earlier than the rest of the country, so now may be a good time to buy here. Prices are expected to start jumping upward by mid-2007.

Caution: Time will tell whether southern New Hampshire can buck the trend of New Englanders moving south for warmer climates.

Ft. Collins, Colorado

Projected single-family home appreciation over five years: 28%

Median home price:
2006 $196,000
2011 $251,000

Population:
2006   278,000
2011   306,000

Per capita income:
2006 $36,600
2011 $48,400

Key information:

- Ft. Collins often appears on "best places" lists in the media—best place to live, best place to retire, best place to raise a family, and best "dream" town. *Money* magazine, for example, rated it as the best small city in America, citing its good schools, low crime, and good jobs in a high-tech economy. The city's recreation is nothing to sneeze at either, with 40 parks, over 60 miles of hiking and biking trails, three city-owned golf courses, and nearby whitewater rafting, kayaking, fishing, and skiing. In addition, it's home to Colorado State University.
- According to Andrew Leventis of the Office of Federal Housing Enterprise Oversight, Colorado housing prices have lagged the rest of the country in recent years, and have had "relatively anemic" appreciation.
- Expect an influx of high-tech companies leaving expensive Silicon Valley, bringing California émigrés with them.

Caution: Another technology slowdown could dampen the rosy housing outlook. Since large divisions of Hewlett-Packard and Eastman Kodak are based here, the economy leans on growth in the tech industry.

Atlanta, Georgia

Projected single-family home appreciation over five years: 24%

Median home price:
2006 $173,000
2011 $214,000

Population:
2006   5,030,000
2011   5,615,000

Per capita income:
2006 $36,000
2011 $45,400

Key information:
*   While the city proper includes only 400,000 residents, the metropolitan area includes 110 municipalities, all vying to outgrow each other. Because commuters outside the I-285 perimeter are having a harder time getting into the city each day, prices inside the beltway are escalating, especially in good neighborhoods in North Atlanta (especially swank areas such as Buckhead) and Peachtree City, located on the perimeter's southern fringe.

Caution: Atlanta housing historically has not appreciated very well, and plant closures for Ford (in 2006) in Hapeville, and General Motors (scheduled for 2008) in Doraville, will not help.

Personal note: Atlanta's traffic is notoriously bad. I lived in Buckhead in the late 1980s and even then couldn't imagine living near or beyond the I-285 perimeter. I can't imagine how bad it is now. Prices in good neighborhoods within a 25-minute commute to downtown would have to boom, one would think.

ADDITIONAL MARKETS AND INDICATORS

Another way to analyze housing market risk is to look at inventory of homes on the market, employment, and mortgage loan payments overdue. Appendix B analyzes selected major markets based on indicators of housing inventory and employment outlook.

WHERE *NOT* TO BUY A HOUSE

The June 12, 2006, National City Corp./Global Insight survey also released the most overvalued home price markets. The worst five markets were as follows:

Area	Median Price (Q1, 2006)	Percent Overvalued (Q1, 2006)
1. Naples, FL	$383,000	102.6%
2. Salinas, CA	$608,600	79.1%
3. Port St. Lucie, FL	$240,800	77.4%
4. Merced, CA	$291,300	77.0%
5. Bend, OR	$276,100	76.4%

The Fiserv/Moody's Economy.com forecasters also predicted that some of the most superheated markets of the past five years, such as Santa Barbara (where the median house costs $638,000) and Las Vegas, will remain flat or fall slightly. Here are their bottom ten markets for June 2006 through June 2007:

City	June 2006–June 2007 Forecast
1. Santa Barbara, CA	–3%
2. Las Vegas, NV	–3%
3. Carson City, NV	–2%
4. Nassau-Suffolk, NY	–2%
5. Greeley, CO	–1%
6. Salinas, CA	0%
7. Stockton, CA	0%
8. Providence, RI	0%
9. Yuma, AZ	0%
10. Pascagoula, MS	0%

The *Business 2.0* magazine study released on October 26, 2006, also provided a bottom ten markets list. This list projects market drops from October 2006 to October 2007:

City	Price Gain 2004–2005	October 2006– October 2007 Forecast
1. Stockton, CA	30.0%	–9.7%
2. Merced, CA	34.7%	–8.9%
3. Reno/Sparks, NV	25/24.4%	–8.9%
4. Fresno, CA	26.9%	–7.9%
5. Vallejo/Fairfield, CA	18.4/25.6%	–7.8%
6. Las Vegas, NV	11.2%	–7.1%
7. Bakersfield, CA	42.8%	–6.6%
8. Sacramento, CA	19.8%	–6.4%
9. Washington, D.C.	16.9%	–6.3%
10. Tucson, AZ	22.0%	–6.2%

Only two cities, Las Vegas and Stockton, California, appeared on both the Fiserv and *Business 2.0* lists. Notice, however, the difference in projections; the Fiserv/Moody's Economy.com list projects Stockton with a 0 percent change from June 2006 to June 2007, while the *Business 2.0* list, which also consulted Moody's Economy.com, projected the prices in Stockton to drop almost 10 percent. Fiserv projects that Las Vegas will have a 3 percent drop, while *Business 2.0* suggests that it will be a 7.1 percent drop. Obviously, these studies have a large margin of error. One thing is clear: Stockton and Las Vegas would not be a great place to invest in single-family homes right now. But even the experts disagree on the other eight bottom markets for single-family housing.

Another way to look at projections is on a worst-case basis. If you are an investor in single-family homes, pay attention to Figure 10.1. Moody's Economy.com also analyzed 379 markets and estimated a worst-case scenario—if you bought at the top of the boom market and sold at the bottom of the slump or crash (depending on how you define your terms) market. Their research forecast the 100 markets most at risk for a price decline, projecting out to 2010.[2]

Notice that all but two of the markets from the Fiserv and *Business 2.0* lists made this list of Moody's Economy.com top 100 most at risk markets. However, Yuma and Pascagoula, being very small markets, may not have been considered in this list of 100.

Now before you get too worked up over these cities, keep the following points in mind:

- Many of these cities experienced 20 percent annual gains over most of the boom years. To stay flat or lose 5, 10, or even 18 percent from peak to bottom is hardly a worry. Their net gain from 2002 might well be over 60 percent.
- These are prices for houses only. This research is not for residential multifamily, commercial, or industrial properties.
- These statistics do not consider what investors do—buy under market, improve properties, and receive rents and tax benefits. If you invest now in a duplex, triplex, or quad in Santa Barbara or Las Vegas, for example, improve the property and increase the rents, you have *forced* the value up. And that is not guesswork or prognostication. Residential multifamily units are valued based on the GRM. If you are able to increase the rents, your property value goes up. It is possible that the going GRM could go down based on the overall market, but probably not dramatically so in a year's time.
- These slight variations up or down in the market are really irrelevant to the buy-and-hold investor.

If you understand basic real estate investing, these numbers should not scare you away from investing, even in these markets,

FIGURE 10.1 *Moody's Home Price Forecast: The 100 Markets Most at Risk to a Price Decline*

Area	State	Peak to Bottom Home Price Decline (%)	Peak	Bottom
Cape Coral	FL	−18.6%	Q4 2005	Q2 2007
Reno	NV	−17.2	Q4 2005	Q4 2008
Merced	CA	−16.1	Q4 2005	Q2 2009
Stockton	CA	−15.7	Q4 2005	Q4 2008
Sarasota	FL	−14.0	Q4 2005	Q3 2007
Naples	FL	−13.8	Q4 2005	Q3 2007
Tucson	AZ	−13.4	Q1 2006	Q2 2008
Las Vegas	NV	−12.9	Q4 2005	Q2 2009
Chico	CA	−12.6	Q4 2005	Q2 2008
Fresno	CA	−12.5	Q1 2006	Q2 2009
Atlantic City	NJ	−12.2	Q4 2005	Q2 2008
Vallejo	CA	−12.1	Q4 2005	Q2 2009
Washington	DC	−12.0	Q4 2005	Q2 2008
Redding	CA	−11.8	Q1 2006	Q2 2008
Detroit	MI	−11.7	Q3 2005	Q4 2006
Riverside	CA	−11.4	Q1 2006	Q4 2008
Bloomington	IL	−11.1	Q3 2005	Q4 2006
Bakersfield	CA	−11.1	Q1 2006	Q2 2009
Greeley	CO	−10.7	Q1 2006	Q2 2008
Salinas	CA	−10.3	Q4 2005	Q2 2008
Santa Ana	CA	−10.0	Q1 2006	Q4 2008
Sacramento	CA	−9.9	Q4 2005	Q2 2008
Carson City	NV	−9.8	Q1 2006	Q2 2009
Phoenix	AZ	−9.3	Q1 2006	Q2 2008
Punta Gorda	FL	−8.9	Q1 2006	Q2 2007
San Diego	CA	−8.5	Q4 2005	Q2 2008
Warren	MI	−8.4	Q3 2005	Q4 2006
Allentown	PA	−8.2	Q4 2005	Q2 2008
Nassau	NY	−8.1	Q1 2006	Q2 2008
Fort Walton Beach	FL	−7.9	Q2 2005	Q3 2006
Santa Rosa	CA	−7.9	Q4 2005	Q2 2008
Ocean City	NJ	−7.6	Q1 2007	Q2 2010
Visalia	CA	−7.3	Q4 2005	Q4 2008
Rockford	IL	−7.3	Q1 2006	Q1 2009
Santa Barbara	CA	−7.2	Q4 2005	Q2 2008

FIGURE 10.1 *Moody's Home Price Forecast: The 100 Markets Most at Risk to a Price Decline (continued)*

Area	State	Peak to Bottom Home Price Decline (%)	Peak	Bottom
Worcester	MA	−7.0%	Q4 2005	Q2 2007
New Orleans	LA	−6.7	Q4 2005	Q3 2007
Saginaw	MI	−6.5	Q1 2006	Q2 2009
Oakland	CA	−6.4	Q4 2005	Q2 2008
Fort Collins	CO	−6.1	Q3 2005	Q2 2007
Portland	ME	−5.9	Q1 2006	Q1 2007
Fort Lauderdale	FL	−5.9	Q4 2005	Q3 2007
West Palm Beach	FL	−5.7	Q4 2005	Q3 2006
Miami	FL	−5.5	Q1 2006	Q2 2008
Edison	NJ	−5.2	Q1 2006	Q2 2008
Los Angeles	CA	−4.8	Q2 2006	Q4 2008
Denver	CO	−4.6	Q2 2006	Q2 2008
Napa	CA	−3.8	Q1 2006	Q3 2006
Providence	RI	−3.6	Q3 2005	Q2 2007
New York	NY	−3.5	Q2 2006	Q4 2008
Champaign	IL	−3.5	Q4 2005	Q1 2009
Essex County	MA	−3.1	Q3 2005	Q3 2006
Bethesda	MD	−3.0	Q4 2005	Q2 2008
Boulder	CO	−2.8	Q4 2005	Q3 2006
Yuba City	CA	−2.6	Q4 2005	Q3 2006
Salt Lake City	UT	−2.3	Q1 2006	Q3 2006
Boston	MA	−2.2	Q2 2006	Q3 2006
Pueblo	CO	−2.1	Q1 2006	Q3 2006
Prescott	AZ	−2.0	Q1 2006	Q2 2008
Madera	CA	−1.8	Q1 2007	Q2 2009
Colorado Springs	CO	−1.6	Q2 2006	Q3 2006
Grand Junction	CO	−1.3	Q2 2006	Q3 2006
Portland	OR	−0.8	Q3 2007	Q2 2009
Lewiston	ID	−0.8	Q1 2007	Q2 2008
St. George	UT	−0.5	Q3 2007	Q2 2008
Honolulu	HI	−0.3	Q2 2007	Q4 2008
Milwaukee	WI	−0.3	Q2 2007	Q3 2008
Hagerstown	MD	−0.2	Q3 2007	Q2 2008
Medford	OR	−0.2	Q3 2007	Q2 2008
San Jose	CA	−0.2	Q1 2007	Q2 2007

Source: Moody's Economy.com

for a number of reasons. First, you could very well use these projections as guides on when to buy. For example, if you are thinking about investing in the Cape Coral market, if this study is correct, the market bottom will arrive in the second quarter of 2007. If you buy a property at that time, you'll be purchasing at almost a 20 percent discount to the peak in the fourth quarter of 2005. Notice that many markets are poised for a price bottom in late 2007, 2008, or 2009. These market bottoms would be ideal times to invest in single-family homes.

Second, if you invest in single-family homes, you are likely one who buys "fixers" and "flips" them. A 2- to 3-year trend doesn't affect you. You are in and out in just a few months. If you invest in single-family homes to rent, this shouldn't bother you either; you should be a buy-and-hold investor and hold the property for 5, 10, or even 20 years or more. If you can afford your mortgage terms when you buy the property, who cares what the comparable sales are in 12 months? That doesn't affect your cash flow or your long-term plan.

Likewise, if you invest in residential multifamily properties, this shouldn't bother you too much either. You are not buying single-family homes. You are buying duplexes, triplexes, and quads. The market is not identical. You are far more concerned about interest rates and the going GRM for your area than what sales figures are for single-family homes. The same goes for commercial properties; you are paying attention to interest and cap rates.

In addition, regardless of what type of property you are investing in, you are improving the property. This is done either through rehab, increased rents, or both. As such, you are forcing the value up. Pay attention to your properties and rates, and buy in good locations. What happens in the single-family home market is not your primary focus.

RESIDENTIAL MULTIFAMILY PROPERTIES

If you are thinking about investing in residential multifamily properties, my suggestion is to invest close to your home if the numbers will work. If they will not work, see if you can find a city close by that will cash-flow (unless, of course, you are a pure location/buy-and-hold investor and don't mind negative cash flow to get a great location). That's what I'm doing now. The GRM rates for the downtown areas of Orlando are far too high to think about cash flow. Because I have some negative cash flow on well-located properties now, I'm looking to balance my portfolio to add some cash flow (sacrificing some appreciation, of course).

The key here is to look at the GRM for your entire market area and determine if the property will cash-flow. For the first time, I'm looking outside my core market. And while the single-family home markets will not be identical to prices for duplexes, triplexes, and quads, the general trend may be the same. As such, I'm paying attention to up-and-coming markets close to me such as Lakeland.

I'm carefully watching prices and the GRM in my core Orlando downtown market. If the prices and GRM don't come down to where I can cash-flow good properties, I'll invest elsewhere. My guess is that the bottom for Orlando may be early to mid-2007. Until then, I may "keep the powder dry."

FORECLOSURES

In recent years, investing in foreclosures has been one of the most popular real estate activities. In times of a downturn, bust, or crash, this type of investing may be even more common. If you are interested in this category of real estate investing, see Figure 10.2, which sets forth the top ten foreclosure markets.

FIGURE 10.2 *The Top Ten Foreclosure Markets*

Market	Median Home Price	Portion of Households in Foreclosure	Comments
Greeley, CO	$163,700	0.59%	Aggressive residential development, risky loan underwriting, and stagnant wages have given this market a foreclosure rate about seven times the national average.
Detroit	$118,800	0.51	The auto industry is hurting, and Ford announced a $5.8 billion quarterly loss for Q3, 2006.
Miami	349,900	0.37	High boom prices, speculation, and rising property insurance premiums have contributed to increased foreclosures.
Indianapolis	123,000	0.35	The city has suffered economic setbacks, which have hurt housing prices.
Ft. Lauderdale	360,800	0.34	Increase in foreclosures since January 2006: 118.5%
Denver	246,300	0.33	The impact from job losses in the telecommunications industry and overbuilding during the boom has taken its toll on Denver.
Dayton, OH	117,400	0.33	Some suggest that lax state regulations made Ohio homeowners susceptible to predatory lenders.
Dallas	156,100	0.31	Lax regulatory controls allowed overdevelopment of residential property and caused an oversupply of inventory, making it difficult to sell existing homes.
Ft. Worth	125,900	0.31	Stagnated income and increasing property taxes have contributed to foreclosures.
Atlanta	166,800	0.30	Corporate layoffs, cuts in pension plans, and upward adjustments in ARM mortgages have increased foreclosures here.

Sources: RealtyTrac and CNNMoney.com, October 25, 2006

RESORT PROPERTIES

You may remember Mark Twain's maxim, "Buy land. They've stopped making it." This truism is even more applicable when we speak about resort properties, especially beachfront properties.

You may be familiar with snow skiing resorts in Colorado or Utah, or mountain cabins in North Carolina. Growing up in Florida, I'm very familiar with most of the beaches in my state, on both coasts. There's not much undeveloped beachfront land on nice beaches, which creates a supply/demand imbalance.

I started going over to my favorite beach, New Smyrna Beach, Florida, when I was in high school. I always loved it—warm water and a wide, clean beach. Around 2000, I went over to New Smyrna to look at beachfront condos. I had a particular complex in mind, Castle Reef. It was in the no-drive area of the beach, but was right across from the only grocery store on A1A, and was within walking distance to the only beachfront restaurant, Chase's. My broker told me about a unit that wasn't officially on the market but said that she knew the owner was thinking of selling it. It was a two-bedroom, two-bath unit right on the ocean—about as close as you can be to the water. And it had recently been designer decorated. My broker thought I could get it for between $265,000 and $275,000. I put in an offer of $264,000, even though it wasn't on the market. Turns out, the owner wanted to sell, but the owner's dad wanted him to keep it so he (dad) could use it in the winter. Dad prevailed.

I returned to shop for condos in this complex in the spring of 2004. I was shocked at the prices. Units on the "bulkhead" part of the complex (closest to the water) had skyrocketed to between $549,000 and $575,000. I cringed, knowing that the fair market value just four years earlier was half of that. Welcome to the beach. So I bought what I thought was another great two-bedroom, two-bath unit, not as close to the water but just behind the pool deck on the ground floor, for $392,000 (you can see it at *www.vrbo.com/80503*). The white-hot appreciation has cooled for these units too, but they won't drop much in value, I can assure you. New Smyrna has no undeveloped land for more units, and therefore supply is capped. Time and baby boomers will continue to force appreciation.

You may know of similar great areas where you live. I know that Florida beach areas such as Sarasota, West Palm Beach, Marco Island, Sanibel Island, and Captiva Island have similar supply issues. I have friends who own town homes in Park City, Utah, that speak of similar supply and building constraints. While most of these resort-type properties will not provide cash flow initially, they do appreciate well and the family time there is, well, priceless.

There's a fair amount of research data suggesting that these second home and beach and resort properties will continue to appreciate well. Consider these influencing factors.

- *Aging population.* The nation continues to age, which means that the largest pool of second home and resort property buyers continues to grow. According to the Census Bureau, by 2011 almost 4 million Americans will turn age 65, a 73 percent increase over the number who reached that age in 2001. In 10 to 15 years, 73 million baby boomers will begin retiring. Every year more baby boomers enter the second home/vacation property market. This demographic trend is driving prices up now because many of the boomers (myself included) are not waiting for retirement to buy a second home. Since vacation homes are somewhat limited in supply, while demand continues to grow, prices will continue to increase. I've seen it firsthand in my favorite beach area. And the supply-to-demand ratio will become even more constricted in properties situated in warm, beach-front locations.

- *Increasing rental rates.* This demographic trend has also been pushing up rental rates for these properties. On average, rental rates nationally have been increasing at 3 to 5 percent annually. This increases income to a property owner who will rent out the unit or house part of the year, which makes it easier to afford. In turn, the greater affordability increases the potential pool of buyers, driving demand even higher. Add to this the fact that advances in health care are allowing Americans to live longer, which also adds to the pool of retiree buyers.

- *Capital gains tax incentives.* The capital gains tax exemption on the sale of a personal residence ($250,000 for individuals and $500,000 for married couples), enacted with the 1997 tax code changes, gave a boost to buyers of second homes and vacation homes. The exemption has allowed many empty nesters to sell their large home (you don't need those extra bedrooms with the kids gone, right?), downsize to a smaller primary residence, and use some of their tax-free gain to buy a second home or vacation home.
- *Use of boom equity.* The single-family home real estate boom from 2000 to 2005 created an enormous amount of equity in many homes. As a result, many people are tapping the equity in their primary residences (either through refinancing or home equity loans or home equity lines of credit) to make down payments for second homes or vacation homes.

The good news if you are thinking about buying a second home or vacation home as an investment is this: the property should appreciate very well. The bad news is that prices are rising faster than income. If you are thinking about waiting until you save up more money, or until we hit a market bottom, don't. If you don't buy quickly, you may not be able to afford it later. Chances are, prices will be considerably more in 2008 or 2009 and beyond.

In July 2004, *SmartMoney* magazine listed ten of the most popular resort locations and compared them with their less-expensive neighbors. Properties located in the less popular locations are typically 20 to 40 percent cheaper than their well-known neighbors. While 2007 prices will certainly be higher than these figures, Figure 10.3 shows the level of bargains for alternative properties.

FIGURE 10.3 *Less Expensive Alternatives for Second Homes or Vacation Homes*

Traditional Resort	2004 Average Price	Alternative	2004 Average Price
Aspen, CO	$450,000	Crested Butte, CO	$320,000
Kiawah Island, SC	350,000	Charleston, SC	165,000
Hamptons, NY	660,000	Shelter Island, NY	550,000
Hilton Head, SC	375,000	Beaufort, SC	200,000
Naples, FL	235,000	Ft. Meyers, FL	170,000
Outer Banks, NC	460,000	Ocean Isle Beach, NC	350,000
Palm Beach, FL	460,000	Vero Beach, FL	155,000
Palm Desert, CA	320,000	Palm Springs, CA	250,000
Park City, UT	600,000	Alta, UT	250,000
Scottsdale, AZ	265,000	Tempe, AZ	150,000

Since I live and grew up in Florida, I can provide a similar list of alternatives to the popular Florida resorts:

Popular Resorts	Alternative(s)
Daytona Beach	Ormond Beach, Palm Coast
Panama City Beach	Destin Beach
Sarasota	Venice
Marco Island	Ft. Meyers
St. Augustine	Crescent Beach

STUDENT HOUSING

In 2006, my publisher released a book about investing in student housing. That's not my forte, and I have not read the book, but investing in student housing is becoming more popular. Buying inexpensive houses, duplexes, triplexes, quads, condos, and town homes near universities and colleges is generally a great idea because you have a constant demand for inexpensive housing. Student housing is particularly enticing now for two reasons. First, available student housing is shrinking. Many public universities have had budget limitations in recent years and have not been able to fund additional housing or dorm upgrades. Second, demand is increasing as universities and colleges have witnessed a dramatic increase in admissions, particularly from echo boomers (children of baby boomers).

YOU HAVE TO START

In this book I've tried to give you the most relevant information for deciding for yourself where the real estate market is going, what type of real estate investing is the safest, how to position yourself in each market, how to evaluate and buy properties, and where to invest. Many of you may be overwhelmed at this point. You've seen too much data and you may suffer from analysis paralysis. If so, take a week off, let your brain relax, and then start looking for something to buy. If you don't have much money to work with, start with a duplex. Ideally, start by investing close to home. But get started so that you can gain experience and get that appreciation and equity buildup clock rolling.

One of the best motivational speakers I've ever heard is the famous insurance guru, Art Williams (founder of A. L. Williams). Upon hearing of people being scared or unable to get off the dime, or being intimidated by being a beginner, Williams liked to say, "Before you can be good, you have to be bad. But before you can be bad, you have to try." To that, I say, just try. Real estate investing, especially residential investing, is not rocket science. If you've made it to the end of this book, you have enough diligence to do this successfully. Trust me.

APPRECIATION RATES
FOR 148 MARKETS

FIGURE A.1   *Appreciation Rates for 148 Markets, Third Quarter 2006*

Metro Area*	State	Median Price (000s)	% Change (1-yr)
Salem	OR	$228.0	24.7%
Elmira	NY	93.6	21.4
Salt Lake City	UT	216.3	19.2
Virginia Beach-Norfolk-Newport News	VA-NC	243.8	16.9
Gainesville	FL	215.2	15.9
Gulfport-Biloxi	MS	154.4	15.7
Wichita	KS	127.9	15.0
Seattle-Tacoma-Bellevue	WA	372.4	14.6
El Paso	TX	129.9	14.3
Baton Rouge	LA	178.4	14.1
Spokane	WA	191.1	14.1
Beaumont-Port Arthur	TX	117.1	12.9
Farmington	NM	176.2	12.9
Durham	NC	176.0	12.5
Eugene-Springfield	OR	234.8	12.4
Portland-Vancouver-Beaverton	OR-WA	285.0	12.3
Atlantic City	NJ	277.2	12.0
Cumberland	MD-WV	100.9	11.9
Albuquerque	NM	191.1	11.9
Dover	DE	214.8	10.6
Binghamton	NY	107.4	10.0
Tulsa	OK	134.9	9.6
Tampa-St.Petersburg-Clearwater	FL	234.0	9.6
Jackson	MS	148.7	8.9
Amarillo	TX	120.8	8.7
Raleigh-Cary	NC	213.5	7.9
Richmond	VA	231.4	7.9
New Orleans-Metairie-Kenner	LA	174.5	7.6
Bismarck	ND	140.4	7.4
NY: Edison	NJ	415.1	7.3
Charleston-North Charleston	SC	216.1	7.0
Trenton-Ewing	NJ	309.8	6.6
San Antonio	TX	146.4	6.4

FIGURE A.1   *Appreciation Rates for 148 Markets, Third Quarter 2006 (continued)*

Metro Area*	State	Median Price (000s)	% Change (1-yr)
Kankakee-Bradley	IL	$138.4	6.1%
Kennewick-Richland-Pasco	WA	166.6	6.0
Greenville	SC	156.3	6.0
Reading	PA	152.3	5.9
Riverside-San Bernardino-Ontario	CA	408.0	5.9
Champaign-Urbana	IL	148.4	5.5
Colordo Springs	CO	224.0	5.5
Houston-Baytown-Sugar Land	TX	152.8	5.3
Los Angeles-Long Beach-Santa Ana	CA	582.0	5.2
Syracuse	NY	124.2	5.1
Knoxville	TN	153.5	5.1
Little Rock-N. Little Rock	AR	128.9	5.1
Oklahoma City	OK	127.0	5.0
Austin-Round Rock	TX	175.5	5.0
Pittsfield	MA	206.0	4.9
Jacksonville	FL	196.1	4.9
New York-Wayne-White Plains	NY-NJ	558.6	4.7
Montgomery	AL	145.9	4.5
Charlotte-Gastonia-Concord	NC-SC	198.3	4.5
Saint Louis	MO-IL	154.4	4.3
Birmingham-Hoover	AL	165.2	4.3
Tallahassee	FL	170.2	4.0
Sioux Falls	SD	140.0	3.9
Springfield	MO	127.0	3.8
San Francisco-Oakland-Fremont	CA	749.4	3.8
Peoria	IL	119.3	3.8
Orlando	FL	271.0	3.7
Topeka	KS	112.3	3.7
New York-Northern New Jersey-Long Island	NY-NJ-PA	477.7	3.6
Louisville	KY-IN	142.5	3.5
Allentown-Bethlehem-Easton	PA-NJ	270.0	3.4
Honolulu	HI	635.0	3.3
Mobile	AL	137.6	3.0

FIGURE A.1   *Appreciation Rates for 148 Markets, Third Quarter 2006 (continued)*

Metro Area*	State	Median Price (000s)	% Change (1-yr)
Buffalo-Niagara Falls	NY	$106.0	3.0%
Atlanta-Sandy Springs-Marietta	GA	176.1	2.9
Dallas-Fort Worth-Arlington	TX	151.3	2.8
Spartanburg	SC	127.9	2.8
Kingston	NY	266.3	2.7
Boulder	CO	366.8	2.6
Glens Falls	NY	164.2	2.6
Albany-Schenectady-Troy	NY	197.6	2.5
Philadelphia-Camden-Wilmington	PA-NJ-DE-MD	236.2	2.4
Cedar Rapids	IA	137.4	2.4
Waterloo/Cedar Falls	IA	113.5	2.3
Madison	WI	227.7	2.2
Yakima	WA	143.6	2.1
NY: Newark-Union	NJ-PA	455.4	1.9
New Haven-Milford	CT	297.4	1.9
Hagerstown-Martinsburg	MD-WV	226.4	1.8
Chicago-Naperville-Joliet	IL	279.4	1.7
Las Vegas-Paradise	NV	318.0	1.6
Rockford	IL	122.3	1.6
Fargo	ND-MN	137.3	1.6
Baltimore-Towson	MD	286.5	1.6
Springfield	IL	113.2	1.5
Rochester	NY	121.8	1.5
Hartford-West Hartford-East Hartford	CT	263.1	1.4
Corpus Christi	TX	130.6	1.4
Omaha	NE-IA	139.9	1.4
Columbia	SC	140.1	1.3
Davenport-Moline-Rock Island	IA-IL	124.9	1.3
Shreveport-Bossier City	LA	132.0	0.7
Greensboro-High Point	NC	151.9	0.7
Springfield	MA	218.8	0.6
Tucson	AZ	243.7	0.6
Decatur	IL	86.0	0.6

Appendix A

FIGURE A.1   *Appreciation Rates for 148 Markets, Third Quarter 2006 (continued)*

Metro Area*	State	Median Price (000s)	% Change (1-yr)
Norwich-New London	CT	$262.1	0.4%
Minneapolis-St. Paul-Bloomington	MN-WI	233.5	0.2
NY: Nassau-Suffolk	NY	471.4	0.1
San Jose-Sunnyvale-Santa Clara	CA	747.4	0.0
Memphis	TN-MS-AR	145.3	–0.1
Chattanooga	TN-GA	136.1	–0.1
Denver-Aurora	CO	253.2	–0.1
Milwaukee-Waukesha-West Allis	WI	219.3	–0.2
Lincoln	NE	138.0	–0.2
Lexington-Fayette	KY	149.0	–0.5
Phoenix-Mesa-Scottsdale	AZ	266.5	–0.6
Kansas City	MO-KS	158.1	–0.6
Gary-Hammond	IN	135.3	–0.7
Anaheim-Santa Ana (Orange Co.)	CA	705.0	–0.8
Pensacola-Ferry Pass-Brent	FL	173.7	–1.0
Des Moines	IA	145.9	–1.3
Charleston	WV	118.5	–1.7
Pittsburgh	PA	120.4	–1.8
Portland-South Portland-Biddeford	ME	244.4	–1.9
San Diego-Carlsbad-San Marcos	CA	601.9	–2.1
Green Bay	WI	151.9	–2.1
Bridgeport-Stamford-Norwalk	CT	466.6	–2.2
Washington-Arlington-Alexandria	DC-VA-MD-WV	431.9	–2.2
Cincinnati-Middletown	OH-KY-IN	144.9	–2.6
Barnstable Town	MA	387.7	–2.7
Grand Rapids	MI	136.6	–2.9
Deltona-Daytona Beach-Ormond Beach	FL	201.5	–3.2
Columbus	OH	151.4	–3.3
Sacramento-Arden-Arcade-Roseville	CA	375.4	–3.5
Worcester	MA	285.4	–3.8
Appleton	WI	127.5	–3.8
Cleveland-Elyria-Mentor	OH	138.5	–4.0
Boston-Cambridge-Quincy	MA-NH**	412.3	–4.3

FIGURE A.1   *Appreciation Rates for 148 Markets, Third Quarter 2006 (continued)*

Metro Area*	State	Median Price (000s)	% Change (1-yr)
Erie	PA	$103.6	−4.4%
Youngstown-Warren-Boardman	OH-PA	86.0	−4.7
Ft. Wayne	IN	101.4	−4.8
Indianapolis	IN	122.4	−5.0
Providence-New Bedford-Fall River	RI-MA	288.2	−5.5
South Bend-Mishawaka	IN	96.0	−5.5
Miami-Fort Lauderdale-Miami Beach	FL	365.1	−5.6
Lansing-E.Lansing	MI	139.8	−6.2
Toledo	OH	115.4	−6.6
Cape Coral-Fort Myers	FL	255.4	−8.0
Akron	OH	118.2	−8.4
Bloomington-Normal	IL	156.3	−8.5
Palm Bay-Melbourne-Titusville	FL	193.6	−9.0
Canton-Massillon	OH	112.3	−9.2
Sarasota-Bradenton-Venice	FL	320.7	−9.4
Detroit-Warren-Livonia	MI	154.1	−10.5
U.S.		224.9	−1.2
NORTHEAST		276.0	−4.8
MIDWEST		170.5	−2.6
SOUTH		187.3	−0.1
WEST		349.0	−0.9

Source: National Association of REALTORS®

Note: California prices provided by the California Association of REALTORS®

* All areas are metropolitan statistical areas (MSA) as defined by the U.S. Office of Management and Budget as of 2004.

** Boston-Cambridge-Quincy, MA-NH — Data from New Hampshire not available.

They include the named central city and surrounding areas. N/A Not Available p Preliminary r Revised

©2006 National Association of REALTORS®

MARKET FORECAST
FOR SELECTED CITIES

The National Association of REALTORS® provides a comprehensive analysis for most of the major metropolitan areas across the United States. NAR identifies five areas of activity in a city that are important to understanding the risks and prospects for the local housing market. These categories are:

1. Price Activity
2. Affordability
3. Home Sales
4. Mortgages
5. Local Fundamentals

Moody's Economy.com also provides three areas of activity helpful in analyzing a market:

1. Rise in Housing Inventory (change from September 30, 2005, to September 30, 2006)
2. Employment Outlook (job growth projections by Moody's Economy.com for two years ending September 30, 2008)
3. Loan Payments Overdue (percentage of mortgage loans 30 days or more delinquent as of the third quarter of 2006)

Appendix B offers a glimpse into these eight areas of activity for 26 metropolitan areas as of July 2006 for NAR figures and as of September 2006 for Moody's Economy.com. Market areas are presented in alphabetical order. Note that these figures are for single-family homes only (not duplexes, triplexes, quads, apartments, or commercial real estate). For a complete analysis and forecast of over 150 metropolitan areas across the nation, I recommend that you go to the NAR Web site, *www.realtor.org/research*.

ATLANTA

	Atlanta	Nation
Prices		
Q1 2005–Q1 2006 appreciation	5.6%	10.3%
3-year price appreciation	14.1%	31.0%
Affordability		
Mortgage debt service/income (Q1 2006)	14.0%	22.0%
Home Sales		
Single-family housing permits (Q1 2006 vs. Q1 2005)	2.0%	-0.9%
Mortgages		
Share of new loans with ARMs (Q1 2006)	33.0%	28.0%
State delinquency rate	5.5%	4.0%
Local Fundamentals		
3-year job growth	3.5%	2.4%
Net migration	71,200	NA
Rise in Housing Inventory	19.0%	NA
Employment Outlook	Average	NA
Loan Payments Overdue	3.83%	2.33%

Comments:

While it has had a relatively high number of foreclosures (good for investors who buy this way), Atlanta seems a fairly safe market in which to invest due to its excellent housing affordability, its strong job growth (57,600 new jobs from Q2 2005 to Q2 2006), and its net migration. The downside for Atlanta has been its below average home appreciation.

BOSTON

	Boston	Nation
Prices		
Q1 2005–Q1 2006 appreciation	–1.5%	10.3%
3-year price appreciation	23.8%	31.0%
Affordability		
Mortgage debt service/income (Q1 2006)	23.8%	22.0%
Home Sales		
Single-family housing permits (Q1 2006 vs. Q1 2005)	–1.0%	–0.9%
Mortgages		
Share of new loans with ARMs (Q1 2006)	30.0%	28.0%
State delinquency rate	3.0%	4.0%
Local Fundamentals		
3-year job growth	–1.8%	2.4%
Net migration	–16,700	NA
Rise in Housing Inventory	22.0%	NA
Employment Outlook	Weak	NA
Loan Payments Overdue	2.20%	2.33%

Comments:

Personally, I would be concerned about a 3-year job loss (–1.8%) to the area, the weak employment outlook, and the loss of 16,700 residents in net migration. However, if you recall from Chapter 6, *Business 2.0* ranked Boston as the number one bubble-proof market in the country. You be the judge. It's also worth noting that Moody's Economy.com figured the third quarter of 2006 to be the bottom for this market (and with only a 2.2% price decline from it's projected peak of the second quarter of 2006).

CHARLOTTE

	Charlotte	Nation
Prices		
Q1 2005–Q1 2006 appreciation	3.0%	10.3%
3-year price appreciation	15.2%	31.0%
Affordability		
Mortgage debt service/income (Q1 2006)	14.1%	22.0%
Home Sales		
Single-family housing permits (Q1 2006 vs. Q1 2005)	21.0%	−2.1%
Mortgages		
Share of new loans with ARMs (Q1 2006)	NA	28.0%
State delinquency rate	4.8%	4.0%
Local Fundamentals		
3-year job growth	2.6%	2.4%
Net migration	34,100	NA
Rise in Housing Inventory	NA	NA
Employment Outlook	Strong	NA
Loan Payments Overdue	3.36%	2.33%

Comments:

While Charlotte has experienced a recent rise in home construction (a 21% increase in housing permits), housing affordability, existing home sales, a significant net migration (34,100), and strong employment outlook figure to make Charlotte a very safe place to invest in single-family homes.

CHICAGO

	Chicago	Nation
Prices		
Q1 2005–Q1 2006 appreciation	11.0%	10.3%
3-year price appreciation	27.8%	31.0%
Affordability		
Mortgage debt service/income (Q1 2006)	20.0%	22.0%
Home Sales		
Single-family housing permits (Q1 2006 vs. Q1 2005)	–1.0%	–0.9%
Mortgages		
Share of new loans with ARMs (Q1 2006)	45.0%	28.0%
State delinquency rate	3.7%	4.0%
Local Fundamentals		
3-year job growth	0.2%	2.4%
Net migration	–28,800	NA
Rise in Housing Inventory	51.0%	NA
Employment Outlook	Average	NA
Loan Payments Overdue	2.30%	2.33%

Comments:

Chicago's high number of ARMs, its significant rise in housing inventory, its low 3-year job growth, and its negative net migration are concerns. However, the 3-year job growth figure is a bit misleading. Chicago lost 41,600 jobs in 2003, but gained 2,600 jobs in 2004 and 46,700 in 2005. With strong job growth, prices may remain stable. In addition, in a city of this size, savvy investors should be able to find deals in any type of real estate.

DALLAS

	Dallas	Nation
Prices		
Q1 2005–Q1 2006 appreciation	4.6%	10.3%
3-year price appreciation	8.9%	31.0%
Affordability		
Mortgage debt service/income (Q1 2006)	11.6%	22.0%
Home Sales		
Single-family housing permits (Q1 2006 vs. Q1 2005)	15.0%	–0.9%
Mortgages		
Share of new loans with ARMs (Q1 2006)	11.0%	28.0%
State delinquency rate	6.2%	4.0%
Local Fundamentals		
3-year job growth	2.2%	2.4%
Net migration	38,000	NA
Rise in Housing Inventory	13.0%	NA
Employment Outlook	Very Strong	NA
Loan Payments Overdue	3.90%	2.33%

Comments:

While the Dallas/Ft Worth area has had meager appreciation, it consistently ranks as one of the most affordable housing markets in the country. With positive numbers for 3-year job growth, a 38,000 net migration, and very strong employment outlook, the Dallas/Ft. Worth area is a fairly safe investment area for homebuyers. These figures suggest that appreciation for home prices should improve over recent years as well.

DENVER

	Denver	Nation
Prices		
Q1 2005–Q1 2006 appreciation	3.5%	10.3%
3-year price appreciation	7.9%	31.0%
Affordability		
Mortgage debt service/income (Q1 2006)	16.8%	22.0%
Home Sales		
Single-family housing permits (Q1 2006 vs. Q1 2005)	–5.0%	–0.9%
Mortgages		
Share of new loans with ARMs (Q1 2006)	39.0%	28.0%
State delinquency rate	3.2%	4.0%
Local Fundamentals		
3-year job growth	2.5%	2.4%
Net migration	11,000	NA
Rise in Housing Inventory	16.0%	NA
Employment Outlook	Strong	NA
Loan Payments Overdue	2.74%	2.33%

Comments:

While Denver has an unusually high level of ARMs, the lack of dramatic price appreciation over the past three years, the home affordability, the decrease in home building, the positive job growth and employment outlook, and the positive net migration suggest that prices here will be stable and have room to increase. However, Moody's Economy.com predicts a 4.6% price decline from Q2 2006 to Q2 2008.

DETROIT

	Detroit	Nation
Prices		
Q1 2005–Q1 2006 appreciation	NA (0.7% in 2005)	10.3%
3-year price appreciation	–0.4%	31.0%
Affordability		
Mortgage debt service/income (Q1 2006)	12.6%	22.0%
Home Sales		
Single-family housing permits (Q1 2006 vs. Q1 2005)	–43.0%	–0.9%
Mortgages		
Share of new loans with ARMs (Q1 2006)	24.0%	28.0%
State delinquency rate	5.8%	4.0%
Local Fundamentals		
3-year job growth	–2.3%	2.4%
Net migration	–25,300	NA
Rise in Housing Inventory	38.0%	NA
Employment Outlook	Very Weak	NA
Loan Payments Overdue	3.94%	2.33%

Comments:

For the single-family home investor, Detroit is a problem. While the market does not present the problem of a bubble-burst (it missed the boom in the first place) and housing is affordable, the job situation is a disaster. From 2001 through 2005, the city lost 165,600 jobs. The slide continues, as unemployed workers move elsewhere, more loans become delinquent, and little building goes on. Moody's Economy.com predicted an 11.7% drop in prices from the peak (projected at Q3 2005) to the bottom (projected at Q4 2006), so perhaps it will rebound from here. For "bottom fishers," this would be the perfect time to buy. While some may be leaving the city, others will be seeking cheaper housing costs, which they'll find in lower priced apartments.

HOUSTON

	Houston	Nation
Prices		
Q1 2005–Q1 2006 appreciation	3.0%	10.3%
3-year price appreciation	8.7%	31.0%
Affordability		
Mortgage debt service/income (Q1 2006)	10.9%	22.0%
Home Sales		
Single-family housing permits (Q1 2006 vs. Q1 2005)	11.0%	–0.9%
Mortgages		
Share of new loans with ARMs (Q1 2006)	11.0%	28.0%
State delinquency rate	6.2 %	4.0%
Local Fundamentals		
3-year job growth	2.7%	2.4%
Net migration	43,600	NA
Rise in Housing Inventory	5.0%	NA
Employment Outlook	Very Strong	NA
Loan Payments Overdue	2.92%	2.33%

Comments:

Houston, like Dallas, largely missed the housing boom, so there's no price bubble to burst. Given the large number of housing permits, the added housing will not help, but there was only a 5% rise in housing inventory last year. The market faces little risk of much of a price decline, and may see price appreciation soon, given the strong employment outlook (68,000 new jobs last year), the net migration of 43,600, and housing affordability.

JACKSONVILLE

	Jacksonville	Nation
Prices		
Q1 2005–Q1 2006 appreciation	19.0%	10.3%
3-year price appreciation	49.3%	31.0%
Affordability		
Mortgage debt service/income (Q1 2006)	17%	22.0%
Home Sales		
Single-family housing permits (Q1 2006 vs. Q1 2005)	0.0%	−0.9%
Mortgages		
Share of new loans with ARMs (Q1 2006)	NA	28.0%
State delinquency rate	3.4%	4.0%
Local Fundamentals		
3-year job growth	7.9%	2.4%
Net migration	17,900	NA
Rise in Housing Inventory	96.0%	NA
Employment Outlook	Strong	NA
Loan Payments Overdue	2.43%	2.33%

Comments:

Jacksonville, like most of Florida, continues to be a good market for housing. Appreciation has been excellent and the city's affordability, coupled with good job growth and net migration, should result in a stable and strong housing market.

LAS VEGAS

	Las Vegas	Nation
Prices		
Q1 2005–Q1 2006 appreciation	9.2%	10.3%
3-year price appreciation	90.7%	31.0%
Affordability		
Mortgage debt service/income (Q1 2006)	27.1%	22.0%
Home Sales		
Single-family housing permits (Q1 2006 vs. Q1 2005)	20.0%	–0.9%
Mortgages		
Share of new loans with ARMs (Q1 2006)	58.0%	28.0%
State delinquency rate	2.4%	4.0%
Local Fundamentals		
3-year job growth	19.2%	2.4%
Net migration	49,200	NA
Rise in Housing Inventory	66.0%	NA
Employment Outlook	Very Strong	NA
Loan Payments Overdue	3.15%	2.33%

Comments:

Las Vegas has had red-hot price appreciation for single-family homes. In 2004, prices jumped a whopping 46%. That appreciation has cooled, but risk remains. Builders continue to build despite a rise in housing inventory and slowing demand, which could result in an oversupply of homes. The 58% of ARM mortgages seems alarmingly high as well. Moody's Economy.com lists Las Vegas as one of the riskiest markets in the country, expecting a 12.9% drop in prices between peak (projected as Q4 2005) and bottom (projected as Q2 2009). However, the strong employment and net migration may bail the city out of a price bust. From 2001 through 2005, the market added 173,800 new jobs (58,700 in 2005), making it one of the strongest employment centers in the country.

Appendix B

LOS ANGELES

	Los Angeles	Nation
Prices		
Q1 2005–Q1 2006 appreciation	19.1%	10.3%
3-year price appreciation	81.1%	31.0%
Affordability		
Mortgage debt service/income (Q1 2006)	45.1%	22.0%
Home Sales		
Single-family housing permits (Q1 2006 vs. Q1 2005)	–4.0%	–0.9%
Mortgages		
Share of new loans with ARMs (Q1 2006)	63.0%	28.0%
State delinquency rate	1.8%	4.0%
Local Fundamentals		
3-year job growth	1.4%	2.4%
Net migration	–72,100	NA
Rise in Housing Inventory	121.0%	NA
Employment Outlook	Weak	NA
Loan Payments Overdue	1.61%	2.33%

Comments:

Los Angeles is an interesting market. On the one hand, price appreciation has been incredible over the past few years, and many cannot afford housing. The mortgage debt service/income is over double the national figure, and the number of ARMs is high. Add a weak employment outlook, a loss of 72,100 residents, and a 121% rise in housing inventory, and one would think this market is prime for tanking. On the other hand, the market did add 42,100 jobs in 2004, 53,600 in 2005, and 65,400 in the 12 months from May 2005 to May 2006. Moody's Economy.com doesn't expect that trend to continue, giving it a "weak" employment outlook. Moody's also predicts a 4.8% price decline from the peak (projected as Q2 2006) to the bottom (projected as Q4 2008). However, *Business 2.0* doesn't buy that analysis, naming LA the fourth best bubble-proof market in the country. You be the judge.

MIAMI

	Miami	Nation
Prices		
Q1 2005–Q1 2006 appreciation	11.2%	10.3%
3-year price appreciation	92.7%	31.0%
Affordability		
Mortgage debt service/income (Q1 2006)	30.9%	22.0%
Home Sales		
Single-family housing permits (Q1 2006 vs. Q1 2005)	–7.0%	–0.9%
Mortgages		
Share of new loans with ARMs (Q1 2006)	43.0%	28.0%
State delinquency rate	3.4%	4.0%
Local Fundamentals		
3-year job growth	7.4%	2.4%
Net migration	38,600	NA
Rise in Housing Inventory	177.0%	NA
Employment Outlook	Strong	NA
Loan Payments Overdue	2.38%	2.33%

Comments:

Miami has had phenomenal price appreciation over the past few years, but that will not continue. In Florida, it's well known that Miami had a tremendous number of speculative investors buying condos, assuming they could hold for a few months and sell at a nice gain. But the music stopped, and many are left with either taking a loss or accepting negative cash flow if they rent. The high mortgage debt service/income ratio and the large number of ARMs reveal that prices are extremely high. Moody's Economy.com expects prices to decline 5.5% from the peak (projected as Q1 2006) to the bottom (projected as Q2 2008). On the positive side, excellent job growth (67,100 in 2004 and 90,300 in 2005), employment outlook, and net migration may soon bail the city out of its present risky situation.

MINNEAPOLIS/ST. PAUL

	Minneapolis	Nation
Prices		
Q1 2005–Q1 2006 appreciation	7.4%	10.3%
3-year price appreciation	25.1%	31.0%
Affordability		
Mortgage debt service/income (Q1 2006)	16.1%	22.0%
Home Sales		
Single-family housing permits (Q1 2006 vs. Q1 2005)	–4.0%	–0.9%
Mortgages		
Share of new loans with ARMs (Q1 2006)	34.0%	28.0%
State delinquency rate	2.6%	4.0%
Local Fundamentals		
3-year job growth	2.0%	2.4%
Net migration	3,000	NA
Rise in Housing Inventory	27.0%	NA
Employment Outlook	Average	NA
Loan Payments Overdue	2.33%	2.33%

Comments:

What can we say other than that Minneapolis/St. Paul seems to be average in just about every category. No big upside, no big downside.

NASHVILLE

	Nashville	Nation
Prices		
Q1 2005–Q1 2006 appreciation	8.7 %	10.3%
3-year price appreciation	17.7%	31.0%
Affordability		
Mortgage debt service/income (Q1 2006)	13.3%	22.0%
Home Sales		
Single-family housing permits (Q1 2006 vs. Q1 2005)	6.0%	–0.9%
Mortgages		
Share of new loans with ARMs (Q1 2006)	NA	28.0%
State delinquency rate	5.7%	4.0%
Local Fundamentals		
3-year job growth	6.5%	2.4%
Net migration	18,800	NA
Rise in Housing Inventory	29.0%	NA
Employment Outlook	Average	NA
Loan Payments Overdue	3.23%	2.33%

Comments:

While Nashville's rise in building permits and housing inventory will thwart too much price appreciation, the job growth over the past few years, coupled with a decent net migration, should prevent much of a price decline. Nashville was *not* one of the 70 markets that Moody's Economy.com predicted to have a price drop in its October 6, 2006 forecast.

NEW YORK

	New York	Nation
Prices		
Q1 2005–Q1 2006 appreciation	15.8%	10.3%
3-year price appreciation	46.0%	31.0%
Affordability		
Mortgage debt service/income (Q1 2006)	35.2%	22.0%
Home Sales		
Single-family housing permits (Q1 2006 vs. Q1 2005)	27.0%	-0.9%
Mortgages		
Share of new loans with ARMs (Q1 2006)	41.0%	28.0%
State delinquency rate	3.4%	4.0%
Local Fundamentals		
3-year job growth	0.6%	2.4%
Net migration	−104,000	NA
Rise in Housing Inventory	47.0%	NA
Employment Outlook	Weak	NA
Loan Payments Overdue	2.22%	2.33%

Comments:

Like Los Angeles, New York has mixed signals. On the one hand, it has had above average appreciation, has very expensive housing (a mortgage debt service/income ratio of 35.2%), a high number of housing permits, ARMs, housing inventory, and lost residents (losing 104,000 in net migration). And while it added 80,700 jobs in the 12 months from July 2005 to July 2006, Moody's Economy.com predicts a weak employment outlook through September 30, 2008. It also predicts a 3.5% price decline from the market's peak (projected as Q2 2006) to the bottom (projected as Q4 2008). Yet, *Business 2.0* projects New York City as the third best bubble-proof market in the country. Go figure.

ORLANDO

	Orlando	Nation
Prices		
Q1 2005–Q1 2006 appreciation	34.0%	10.3%
3-year price appreciation	76.4%	31.0%
Affordability		
Mortgage debt service/income (Q1 2006)	20.4%	22.0%
Home Sales		
Single-family housing permits (Q1 2006 vs. Q1 2005)	6.0%	–0.9%
Mortgages		
Share of new loans with ARMs (Q1 2006)	38.0%	28.0%
State delinquency rate	3.4%	4.0%
Local Fundamentals		
3-year job growth	14.4%	2.4%
Net migration	57,600	NA
Rise in Housing Inventory	133.0%	NA
Employment Outlook	Very Strong	NA
Loan Payments Overdue	2.20%	2.33%

Comments:

Since this is my home market, I know it well. But first, let's look at the numbers. Over the past few years, Orlando has had phenomenal appreciation, especially if you bought homes in good or hot areas. Home price appreciation was 38.4% in 2005 alone. Many have been waiting on a drastic price retrenchment, but it hasn't come. I'm one of those waiting, hoping that I can buy at the very bottom for both a house and apartments. Yes, the market has weakened, and it takes longer to sell. Some have dropped prices by 5% or 10% to get them sold. Others wait and get close to their asking prices. But if you are expecting a 15% drop in good neighborhoods, it isn't going to happen.

Indeed, we could have further softening, as I'm hoping. Housing permits continue to grow, and I know the main builder pulling the largest number of them (and he's not slowing). Orlando has a high number of ARMs and a truckload of houses on the market (inventory), yet prices have held and actually went *up* 3.4% from Q1 2005 to Q1 2006. I know why, because I've lived here most of my life. While some people might vote for San Diego, Orlando is probably the best place in the country to live (not that I'm a little biased, of course!). We have no state income tax, have very affordable housing (notice that the mortgage debt service/income ratio is below the national average), are one hour to either coast (with warm water and some of the world's nicest beaches), and are the number one tourist destination in the world (thank you, Walt Disney). Our economy, net migration, and job outlook (adding 130,600 jobs from 2003 through 2005) are both strong. What more do you want?

If there is a downside, it's this: because of low cap rates, it's almost impossible to buy apartments here (or in any major city in Florida) that will cash-flow from day one. Of course, as I've preached before, buying a quad and living in it or buying in outskirt areas solves that. But that takes all of the fun out!

PHILADELPHIA

	Philadelphia	Nation
Prices		
Q1 2005–Q1 2006 appreciation	14.2%	10.3%
3-year price appreciation	45.5%	31.0%
Affordability		
Mortgage debt service/income (Q1 2006)	15.8%	22.0%
Home Sales		
Single-family housing permits (Q1 2006 vs. Q1 2005)	0.0%	–0.9%
Mortgages		
Share of new loans with ARMs (Q1 2006)	23.0%	28.0%
State delinquency rate	4.6%	4.0%
Local Fundamentals		
3-year job growth	1.3%	2.4%
Net migration	–9,800	NA
Rise in Housing Inventory	34.0%	NA
Employment Outlook	Weak	NA
Loan Payments Overdue	2.19%	2.33%

Comments:

Philadelphia is another city with mixed signals. On the one hand, it has a negative net migration, rising housing inventory, and a weak employment outlook. It has had stable price appreciation, even recently. Prices climbed a robust 14.2% from Q1 2005 to Q1 2006. Homes remain very affordable for the income here. Housing permits are stable. On the other hand, Philly added 17,000 jobs in 2004, 27,600 in 2005, and 34,500 in the 12 months from July 2005 to July 2006. In addition, it was *not* one of the 70 markets that Moody's Economy.com predicted to have a home price drop in its October 6, 2006 forecast. Maybe when Rocky retires the city will lose some of its luster!

PHOENIX

	Phoenix	Nation
Prices		
Q1 2005–Q1 2006 appreciation	38.4%	10.3%
3-year price appreciation	69.0%	31.0%
Affordability		
Mortgage debt service/income (Q1 2006)	24.2%	22.0%
Home Sales		
Single-family housing permits (Q1 2006 vs. Q1 2005)	–14.0%	-0.9%
Mortgages		
Share of new loans with ARMs (Q1 2006)	45.0%	28.0%
State delinquency rate	2.2%	4.0%
Local Fundamentals		
3-year job growth	12.0%	2.4%
Net migration	115,200	NA
Rise in Housing Inventory	146.0%	NA
Employment Outlook	Very Strong	NA
Loan Payments Overdue	1.48%	2.33%

Comments:

Phoenix continues to be a strong market. The market has had blistering appreciation, and the rise in inventory and large number of ARMs would seem to indicate that a correction is still due. Indeed, Moody's Economy.com predicts a 9.3% drop in prices from market peak (projected as Q1 2006) to bottom (projected as Q2 2008). Nonetheless, other fundamentals are very strong. The net migration of 115,200 indicates that many people still flee the high prices of California for the relatively affordable Phoenix area. More important is the job situation. The market added 191,300 jobs from 2003 through 2005, and the employment outlook going forward is very strong.

RALEIGH-DURHAM

	Raleigh/Durham	Nation
Prices		
Q1 2005–Q1 2006 appreciation	3.6/1.6%	10.3%
3-year price appreciation	18.9/12.8%	31.0%
Affordability		
Mortgage debt service/income (Q1 2006)	16.3/13.9%	22.0%
Home Sales		
Single-family housing permits (Q1 2006 vs. Q1 2005)	16/9.0%	−0.9%
Mortgages		
Share of new loans with ARMs (Q1 2006)	NA	28.0%
State delinquency rate	4.8%	4.0%
Local Fundamentals		
3-year job growth	7.4/−0.6%	2.4%
Net migration	25,600/2,600	NA
Rise in Housing Inventory	9.0%	NA
Employment Outlook	Strong	NA
Loan Payments Overdue	2.16%	2.33%

Comments:

The Raleigh-Durham area is another area where price appreciation has been anemic, but the market has very affordable housing. Raleigh, with better appreciation, job growth, and net migration, is the stronger of the two cities. For both the single-family home and apartment investor, this is a classic market that will give you good cash flow but anemic appreciation.

SACRAMENTO

	Sacramento	Nation
Prices		
Q1 2005–Q1 2006 appreciation	6.7%	10.3%
3-year price appreciation	80.3%	31.0%
Affordability		
Mortgage debt service/income (Q1 2006)	31.7%	22.0%
Home Sales		
Single-family housing permits (Q1 2006 vs. Q1 2005)	–36.0%	–0.9%
Mortgages		
Share of new loans with ARMs (Q1 2006)	55.0%	28.0%
State delinquency rate	1.8%	4.0%
Local Fundamentals		
3-year job growth	5.8%	2.4%
Net migration	14,000	NA
Rise in Housing Inventory	47.0%	NA
Employment Outlook	Average	NA
Loan Payments Overdue	2.3%	2.33%

Comments:

Sacramento, like most other California markets, has enjoyed outstanding appreciation during the recent boom. That blistering pace, however, has slowed dramatically. The dramatic decrease in building permits (down 36%) reveals that builders are wary of oversupply. Like most of California, houses are not very affordable here, and this has caused an alarmingly high number of ARMs. Notwithstanding that, however, the market has had a positive net migration and positive job growth since 2001. Moody's Economy.com nevertheless predicts a 9.9% drop in prices from peak (projected as Q4 2005) to bottom (projected as Q2 2008).

ST. LOUIS

	St. Louis	Nation
Prices		
Q1 2005–Q1 2006 appreciation	2.5%	10.3%
3-year price appreciation	19.5%	31.0%
Affordability		
Mortgage debt service/income (Q1 2006)	11.1%	22.0%
Home Sales		
Single-family housing permits (Q1 2006 vs. Q1 2005)	–10.0%	–0.9%
Mortgages		
Share of new loans with ARMs (Q1 2006)	22.0%	28.0%
State delinquency rate	4.4%	4.0%
Local Fundamentals		
3-year job growth	0.4%	2.4%
Net migration	–2,100	NA
Rise in Housing Inventory	31.0%	NA
Employment Outlook	Weak	NA
Loan Payments Overdue	2.83%	2.33%

Comments:

St. Louis is another market where appreciation is slow, but cash flow should be good. The housing is extremely affordable (the median home price in 2005 was only $140,700), with a mortgage debt service/income ratio of one-half of the national average. While the employment outlook is weak, the market did add 7,800 new jobs from Q2 2005 to Q2 2006. That, coupled with a decrease in permits, should protect prices from falling too far here.

SAN DIEGO

	San Diego	Nation
Prices		
Q1 2005–Q1 2006 appreciation	4.0%	10.3%
3-year price appreciation	66.8%	31.0%
Affordability		
Mortgage debt service/income (Q1 2006)	45.0%	22.0%
Home Sales		
Single-family housing permits (Q1 2006 vs. Q1 2005)	–22.0%	–0.9%
Mortgages		
Share of new loans with ARMs (Q1 2006)	59.0%	28.0%
State delinquency rate	1.8%	4.0%
Local Fundamentals		
3-year job growth	4.2%	2.4%
Net migration	–26,500	NA
Rise in Housing Inventory	52.0%	NA
Employment Outlook	Average	NA
Loan Payments Overdue	1.88%	2.33%

Comments:

The blistering price appreciation of San Diego has cooled considerably, and the market is likely to see price declines. The city, while one of the country's most beautiful, is simply too expensive, at least in terms of housing. In 2005, the market's median home price rose to $603,000. With a mortgage debt service/income ratio of 45%, it is more than twice the national average, resulting in an astonishing number of ARMs (59%). Couple that with a negative migration and average employment outlook and the market seems poised for a price correction. Moody's Economy.com predicts an 8.5% drop in prices from peak (projected as Q4 2005) to bottom (projected as Q2 2008).

SAN FRANCISCO

	San Francisco	Nation
Prices		
Q1 2005–Q1 2006 appreciation	5.0%	10.3%
3-year price appreciation	37.9%	31.0%
Affordability		
Mortgage debt service/income (Q1 2006)	41.1%	22.0%
Home Sales		
Single-family housing permits (Q1 2006 vs. Q1 2005)	–14.0%	–0.9%
Mortgages		
Share of new loans with ARMs (Q1 2006)	72.0%	28.0%
State delinquency rate	1.8%	4.0%
Local Fundamentals		
3-year job growth	–2.4%	2.4%
Net migration	–9,300	NA
Rise in Housing Inventory	63.0%	NA
Employment Outlook	Average	NA
Loan Payments Overdue	1.11%	2.33%

Comments:

San Francisco definitely has "issues." Prices of homes here are out of sight (with a median home price in 2005 of $713,400). The mortgage debt service/income ratio is almost double the national average. A shocking 72% of homes have ARMs, indicating that folks cannot afford the payment of a fully amortized fixed-rate loan. People continue to leave the city and the housing inventory rose by 63%. The city lost 165,900 jobs from 2001 through 2004. Nevertheless, prices continue to rise. The market did gain 17,000 jobs in 2005, and Moody's Economy.com did not list it among the 70 cities it projected to have price declines. *Business 2.0* listed it as one of its top five bubble-proof markets. You be the judge.

SEATTLE

	Seattle	Nation
Prices		
Q1 2005–Q1 2006 appreciation	16.4%	10.3%
3-year price appreciation	38.2%	31.0%
Affordability		
Mortgage debt service/income (Q1 2006)	22.9%	22.0%
Home Sales		
Single-family housing permits (Q1 2006 vs. Q1 2005)	4.0%	–0.9%
Mortgages		
Share of new loans with ARMs (Q1 2006)	47.0%	28.0%
State delinquency rate	2.2%	4.0%
Local Fundamentals		
3-year job growth	3.5%	2.4%
Net migration	15,900	NA
Rise in Housing Inventory	37.0%	NA
Employment Outlook	Strong	NA
Loan Payments Overdue	1.36%	2.33%

Comments:

Seattle homes have been appreciating recently as other areas have been depreciating. The appreciation of 16.4% from Q1 2005 to Q1 2006 was well above the national average, and the latest numbers show that appreciation is continuing. Part of that growth may be due to a stall in prices in 2002 (appreciation of only 2.2%) and 2003 (appreciation of only 3.8%). Job growth here has been good since 2004, and the employment outlook is strong. Net migration is positive, and the delinquency rate is very low. This is a strong and stable market.

TAMPA

	Tampa	Nation
Prices		
Q1 2005–Q1 2006 appreciation	20%	10.3%
3-year price appreciation	49.2%	31.0%
Affordability		
Mortgage debt service/income (Q1 2006)	18.4%	22.0%
Home Sales		
Single-family housing permits (Q1 2006 vs. Q1 2005)	−5.0%	−0.9%
Mortgages		
Share of new loans with ARMs (Q1 2006)	36.0%	28.0%
State delinquency rate	3.4%	4.0%
Local Fundamentals		
3-year job growth	9.5%	2.4%
Net migration	58,500	NA
Rise in Housing Inventory	219.0%	NA
Employment Outlook	Strong	NA
Loan Payments Overdue	2.28%	2.33%

Comments:

Appreciation in Tampa, like other Florida markets, has been blistering. In 2005, median home prices jumped 25.1%. That pace will not continue, but significant price drops are also doubtful once this glut of homes is absorbed. But even with the jump in prices, homes here are still very affordable, with the mortgage debt service/ income ratio well below the national average. Tampa was *not* one of Moody's 70 cities expected to see a price drop. That's likely due to the strong employment situation. In 2004 and 2005 alone, the market added over 104,000 new jobs. Couple that with a strong net migration, and the market should remain stable and strong. The downside to this market is that, like most Florida markets, apartment buyers face low cap rates, which means little cash flow.

WASHINGTON, D.C.

	Washington	Nation
Prices		
Q1 2005–Q1 2006 appreciation	11.0%	10.3%
3-year price appreciation	74.9%	31.0%
Affordability		
Mortgage debt service/income (Q1 2006)	25.4%	22.0%
Home Sales		
Single-family housing permits (Q1 2006 vs. Q1 2005)	–13.0%	–0.9%
Mortgages		
Share of new loans with ARMs (Q1 2006)	28.0%	28.0%
State delinquency rate	2.6%	4.0%
Local Fundamentals		
3-year job growth	7.0%	2.4%
Net migration	9,200	NA
Rise in Housing Inventory	69.0%	NA
Employment Outlook	Average	NA
Loan Payments Overdue	1.56%	2.33%

Comments:

There are different views on this market. First, the fundamental numbers don't seem to be abnormal in any category (except for an excellent 3-year appreciation). But Moody's sees the employment outlook as merely average and predicts a significant price drop of 12% from market peak (projected as Q4 2005) to bottom (projected as Q2 2008). However, the NAR sees the job market as exceptionally strong. With 242,600 new jobs added from 2001 through 2005, it's hard to argue with that thought. You be the judge.

Chapter 1

1. John R. Talbott, *The Coming Crash in the Housing Market* (McGraw-Hill, 2003), p. 109.

2. Ibid.

3. National Association of REALTORS®.

4. Zip Realty, as reported in the *Wall Street Journal Online,* October 20, 2006.

5. RealEstateJournal.com, October 11, 2006.

6. "Metro Home Prices Flat," CNNMoney.com, August 21, 2006, as compiled by the National Association of REALTORS®.

Chapter 2

1. John R. Talbott, *Sell Now! The End of the Housing Bubble* (St. Martin's Griffin, 2006), p. 27.

2. John R. Talbott, *The Coming Crash in the Housing Market* (McGraw-Hill, 2003), p. 109.

3. Ibid., p. 117.

4. Ibid., p. 88.

5. Ibid., p. 91.

6. Ibid., pp. 88–89.

7. John Rubino, *How to Profit from the Coming Real Estate Bust* (Rodale, 2003), pp. 2, 114.

8. One exception is the book by David Decker and George Sheldon, *Cash In on the Coming Real Estate Crash* (Wiley, 2006).

9. Talbott, *The Coming Crash in the Housing Market,* p. 35.

Chapter 3

1. Marcel Arsenault, John Hamilton, Ben Leeds, and Gerald Marcil, *How to Build a Real Estate Empire* (Foundations of Wealth Publishing Company, 2005), p. 81.

Chapter 4

1. Marcel Arsenault, John Hamilton, Ben Leeds, and Gerald Marcil, *How to Build a Real Estate Empire* (Foundations of Wealth Publishing Company, 2005), pp. 39–40.

2. Ibid., p. 81.

3. Ibid., pp. 86–87.

4. For a complete analysis of how to use the 1031 exchange, see Chapter 13 ("How to Sell and Pay No Taxes") of my earlier book, *Investing in Duplexes, Triplexes & Quads: The Fastest and Safest Way to Real Estate Wealth* (Kaplan Publishing, 2006).

5. Arsenault, et al., p. 13.

6. Craig Hall, *Timing the Real Estate Market* (McGraw-Hill, 2004), p. 5.

7. Ibid., pp. 5, 23.

8. Ibid., pp. 165–66.

9. Ibid., pp. 247–48.

Chapter 5

1. Marcel Arsenault, John Hamilton, Ben Leeds, and Gerald Marcil (compiled by Marcus, Millichap & Green), *How to Build a Real Estate Empire* (Foundations of Wealth, 2005), p. 159.

2. For a complete understanding of investing in tax liens and tax deeds, see my earlier book, *Profit by Investing in Real Estate Tax Liens* (Kaplan Publishing, 2004).

3. Craig Hall, *Timing the Real Estate Market* (McGraw-Hill, 2004), pp. 5, 23.

Chapter 6

1. RealEstateJournal.com, October 11, 2006.

2. Ibid.

3. See "Investing in Multifamily Property," a report by TIAA-CREF Asset Management, a division of Teachers Advisors, Inc., a registered investment advisor and subsidiary of Teachers Insurance and Annuity Association, Winter 2005.

Chapter 9

1. "Home Prices Keep Sliding; While Hesitant Buyers Sit Tight," RealEsateJournal.com, October 26, 2006.

2. Ibid.

3. Ibid.

4. "Housing Correction Has Further to Run, Realtors Predict," RealEstateJournal.com, November 13, 2006.

5. "Which Makes a Better Investment, a House or a Multifamily Property?" RealEstateJournal.com, February 3, 2006.

6. See David Lereah, *Why the Real Estate Boom Will Not Bust—And How You Can Profit from It* (Currency Doubleday, 2005), pp. 18–19.

7. "Housing Decline Sparks Slowdown in Construction," *Wall Street Journal*, October 27, 2006, A-1, 6.

8. *Orlando Sentinel*, October 27, 2006, A-1, 16.

9. "Home Prices Keep Sliding; While Hesitant Buyers Sit Tight," RealEsateJournal.com, October 26, 2006.

10. "Some Predict That the Worst of the Housing Slump Has Past," RealEstateJournal.com, October 31, 2006.

11. Ibid.

12. "Greenspan: Worst of Housing Woes Are Behind Us," CNNMoney.com, November 6, 2006.

13. "Metrostudy report predicts turnaround in housing market," *Orlando Business Journal*, November 3–9, 2006, p.3.

14. Ibid.

15. RealEstateJournal.com, October 31, 2006.

16. Dataquick, September 2006.

17. "Housing Decline Sparks Slowdown in Construction," *Wall Street Journal,* October 27, 2006, A-1, 6.

18. CNNMoney.com, October 27, 2006.

19. "CBRE multifamily outlook: Investors at the gate," *Orlando Business Journal,* November 10–16, 2006, p. 6.

Chapter 10

1. See CNNMoney.com, October 25, 2006.

2. See CNNMoney.com, October 6, 2006.